A GUIDE TO THE COLLECTIVE AWAKENING

ADVICE, TOOLS & ART PROJECTS

BY JENNA WALKER

From my HEART to yours

◆ FriesenPress

One Printers Way
Altona, MB R0G 0B0
Canada

www.friesenpress.com

Copyright © 2022 by Jenna Walker
First Edition — 2022

Permissions:
The Prophet by Kahlil Gibran. Penguin Random House, Toronto, ON, 2008.
Walden by Henry David Thoreau. Arcturus Publishing Limited, London, 2020.
The Power of Now by Eckhart Tolle. Namaste Publishing, Inc., Vancouver, BC, 2004.
Wheels of Life by Anodea Judith. Llewellyn Publications, MN, USA, 2016."

The author does not offer medical advice, or the use of techniques as a form of treatment for emotional, physical or medical issues without the consultation of a physician. The intent of the author is to offer advice, tools and art projects in a general nature to support the process of awakening and emotional healing based on personal life experiences. In the event you use any of the advice, or attempt any of the art projects mentioned, the author and publisher take on no responsibility for your actions. The FDA has not assessed any of the content in this book.

All rights reserved.

No part of this publication may be reproduced in any form, or by any means, electronic or mechanical, including photocopying, recording, or any information browsing, storage, or retrieval system, without permission in writing from FriesenPress.

ISBN
978-1-03-913657-1 (Hardcover)
978-1-03-913656-4 (Paperback)
978-1-03-913658-8 (eBook)

1. BODY, MIND & SPIRIT, INSPIRATION & PERSONAL GROWTH

Distributed to the trade by The Ingram Book Company

Table of Contents

Foreword — 1

Introduction — 3
- PARTS OF MY JOURNEY — 4
- THE EGO — 9
- THE HIGHER SELF — 11
- THE CHAKRAS — 12
- DIMENSIONS OF CONSCIOUSNESS — 16
- COLLECTIVE AWAKENING — 18
- THE ASCENSION — 20

Chapter 1 THE HUMAN EXPERIENCE AND THE ASCENSION — 23

Chapter 2 THE BODY AND ASCENSION SYMPTOMS — 35
- ESTABLISHING A DEEPER CONNECTION: — 37
- WAYS TO COMMUNICATE WITH THE BODY: — 38
- OUR HANDS FOR SUPPORT — 40
- WHAT ARE SOME ASCENSION SYMPTOMS? — 41
- HOW TO SUPPORT THE BODY DURING ASCENSION SYMPTOMS: — 43
- HOW LONG WILL ASCENSION SYMPTOMS LAST? — 44

Chapter 3 WATER — 49
- WATER FOR DRINKING: — 49
- WATER FOR CLEARING ENERGY: — 52

Chapter 4 FOOD — 61
- HELPFUL TIPS TO CONSIDER: — 62
- LIMIT DAIRY PRODUCTS — 63
- SUGAR — 63
- SET MEAL TIMES — 65

	SUPPLEMENTS	65
	BODY CLEANSES AND FASTING	68
Chapter 5	**MEDITATION AND THE BREATH**	**73**
	THE BREATH	78
	BREATHING TECHNIQUES	78
Chapter 6	**CRYSTALS**	**83**
	CRYSTALS IN DRINKING WATER?!	85
	HOW TO PICK CRYSTALS	86
	CLEANING CRYSTALS	90
	EIGHT WAYS TO CLEAN CRYSTALS:	91
	CHARGING AND PROGRAMMING CRYSTALS	96
	FOUR WAYS TO CHARGE CRYSTALS:	97
	OTHER THINGS TO DO WITH CRYSTALS	98
Chapter 7	**SPIRIT GUIDES**	**103**
Chapter 8	**HEALING MODALITIES**	**111**
	NATURE FOR HEALING	114
	SOUND FOR HEALING	118
Chapter 9	**OTHER TIPS AND TOOLS**	**121**
	PSYCHIC ABILITIES—OUR DIVINE POWERS	121
	SELF-LOVE AND SELF-CARE	122
	GRATITUDE	124
	GROUNDING	125
	CUTTING CORDS	126
Chapter 10	**ART FOR HEALING**	**131**
	PROFESSIONAL OR BEGINNER? IT DOESN'T MATTER	135
	APPROPRIATION IN ART	139
	PROCESS OF EMOTIONAL RELEASE THROUGH CREATIVITY	141
	FOR ALL PROJECTS: SET UP A WORKING SPACE	144
	THE CREATIVE PROCESS FOR EXPRESSION:	145

LOOK AT YOUR PIECE IN DIFFERENT WAYS:	153
JOURNALING AND FREEWRITING OPTION:	153
AFTER WORKING ON A PROJECT	154

Chapter 11　ART PROJECTS — **157**

GENERAL AND OPTIONAL SUPPLIES FOR THE CREATIVE PROCESS:	157
MIXING PAINT AND BRUSH CARE:	159
THROUGHOUT THE CREATIVE PROCESS:	160
PROJECT #1	161
PROJECT #2	162
PROJECT #3	167
PROJECT #4	172
PROJECT #5	178
PROJECT #6	182
PROJECT #7	186
PROJECT #8	192
PROJECT # 9	197
PROJECT #10	202

Conclusion — **209**

Acknowledgements — **213**

Appendix — **215**

Bibliography — **217**

Endnotes — **220**

Foreword

I would like to thank you for acquiring this book and creating the time to read it. It is my hope that you will find some comfort and support in the words I have written. I am not a doctor, dietitian, psychologist, art therapist, scientific expert, or even a writer. I am just a normal human being who has been walking this path of awakening for over twenty years. Throughout my journey, I have encountered deep personal suffering and many moments of utter bliss and connection. I have had life-altering epiphanies, while other life lessons were learned at a slower pace. I have met a great deal of connected people and many others who are not.

Throughout this accumulated experience, I gathered knowledge that has triggered a remembering of my *soul* and the deeper purpose of this lifetime for me. One of my purposes is to be of service to others. I was driven to write this book to offer other's relief and advice based on my personal experiences and the tools that are helping me along my journey. Ultimately, we are all undergoing this awakening process, but it is a unique and individual process. We will all achieve true enlightenment when it is our destined time, though the steps we take to get there will vary according to our own life's journey.

As you read the ideas, advice, and suggestions I offer, please do so with an open heart and an open mind. You do not have to agree with me or follow any of my recommendations. You can do some of the things I suggest or none at all. You may be inspired by what I talk about and have new ideas of your own, or you might want to research something I have mentioned. I recommend acquiring a notebook for you to write stuff down as you read. Alternatively, you can just write or doodle in the blank spaces of this book. I want you to find your own answers, be inspired by more people, and discover music and art that resonate with you. I want you to cultivate your personal journey by following your own intuition. I also want you to enter this reading knowing that a fellow human being, who truly empathizes and understands, is also experiencing this change . . . *you are not alone and you are not going crazy.*

Because this journey of awakening is intense, I feel it's important to mention and emphasize that the tools offered here are not meant to help you get *out* of or *change* the experiences you are undergoing. Instead, they are meant to offer your body, mind, and soul comfort and support *while* you go through this awakening process. Thinking that we have to fix things, change things, and acquire things to make us feel better . . . that is all ego. Following the desires of the ego will not bring us the true happiness, peace, and growth we seek. It will only lead to more things that need fixing, doing, changing, acquiring. Instead, we need to acknowledge, honour, and hold space for what is actually going on in the present moment. Whatever it is that you are experiencing is exactly what you came here to experience, even if you do not remember it. You cannot get this wrong, even when it feels like you are failing. That is just part of the process—*the unravelling of the ego*. Instead of judging, resisting, and turning away from what is happening, we need to give it our focus and face it completely, however hard that may be. We need to feel and embrace the sadness, the pain, the sickness, and the fear and offer it our undivided attention and support. It will eventually pass, but if it is here at the moment, then that is where our attention needs to be.

If you are reading these words, something deeper has brought you here. The divine Universe has nothing but unconditional love for all creations, and that includes you! Many times, when things are tough, we call out for help, but feel like we get no response. But we do! It is just not how we would expect it in this realm of 3D consciousness. We may expect to hear a voice and get answers, get a better job, get revenge or get a bunch of money and think that this will make our lives better or our problems will go away. However, these things will not solve all your problems; the problems are happening for an important reason, and we have to look deeply into them to see. They are triggering a growth, an undoing of social conditioning, and a reawakening of the human consciousness.

Unfortunately, it is through suffering and struggle that our personal awakening is kick-started. Those negative experiences initiate a deep remembering of who we really are and why we are here. The guidance and support of the divine Universe is much quieter and softer than the loud presence of the ego. So, in order to converse with the divine Universe, we need to slow down, quiet our minds, and use all our senses to receive the messages that are coming to us. These messages may come in the form of coincidences or through synchronicities that, to the un-awakened mind, seems like nothing at all. The divine Universe may communicate to you through number patterns, music, books, random people, or subtle thoughts that enter your awareness. If you miss the message in the moment, it will come again in a different way until you recognize it, so no worries about missing out on anything.

With all that being said, I hope that by reading this book and trying the art projects you will find some comfort and support to help you on your journey. Remember: You are not alone and the journey will eventually switch courses. But for now, we are changing, unravelling, reconnecting, growing, and rediscovering who we really are ... *sacred, infinite, powerful, unique, and divine beings of creation.*

Introduction

Before we begin this journey together, there are terms used throughout this book that are not common knowledge among the majority of the planet's population. These terms can be found throughout the history of various cultures around the world. They are also found woven throughout the Arts, cinema, music, books, fashion, and the internet.

I want to share my personal interpretations, as an introduction to these terms, to make following along easier as you read this book. You may have already heard of some of them and have a basic understanding of what they mean. Regardless, please do your own research; there is much for us to remember!

Whenever I mention the word *Universe*, I am referring to:

God, Yahweh, Allah, Jehovah, Father, Holy Spirit, the Creator, the Maker, the Almighty, King of Kings, Supreme Being, Source, Universal Life Force

To me, *spirituality* means:

Finding my pure essence, my spirit. It means reconnecting with my eternal divine Self and being at one with the divine Universe and everything in it. I do not need anyone to facilitate my connection, or explain it to me. It is up to me to grasp it and understand it from my unconscious, conscious, and subconscious state of awareness.

So, what are these terms I speak of? They are the:

- Ego
- Higher Self
- Chakras
- Dimensions of Consciousness
- Collective Awakening
- Ascension

PARTS OF MY JOURNEY

Before I jump into explaining a bit about each of these subjects, let me delve into a little of my past and how I became acquainted with them myself.

Since a very young age, I felt that the majority of what we were being taught and presented with in the Western culture was mostly nonsense, backwards thinking that was based in fear (on the surface it looks good, but we have so much more potential). I was aware of the holes and, sometimes, the missing pieces in the collective stories that society was trying to program us with. By programs, I mean racial segregation, the inequality of the sexes, or the way in which we destroy the very planet that sustains our life and future generations.

As a young girl, I found interactions with most people very confusing and disheartening. Being extremely sensitive and aware of others' feelings and thoughts, many of the things people said or did contradicted the energy I felt radiating from their bodies. These abilities were overwhelming and confusing for me in our current society.

Sadly, I didn't have the support or knowledge to help grow and strengthen these abilities until I became a young adult. Regardless, I continued to believe there was so much more to everything, and I felt our human experience should consist of more love and unity between people, themselves, and our natural surroundings.

I dreamed of a utopian world where there was peace and everyone was striving for their own personal best, whatever that meant to each individual. Unfortunately, I was continually met with opposition, being told I was a dreamer, a hippie, or a conspiracy theorist. Society told me to just follow along with what the majority of the world was doing: *Graduate, get a job, a house, a flashy car, fancy clothes, get married, have kids, go into debt and work, work, work. Do not ask questions, do not think for yourself, and definitely do not follow your heart's desires. Oh, and do not be sensitive and feel too much.*

Well, that just didn't feel right to me or even seem rational or healthy. There has always been this element deep inside of me that knew there is so much more . . . more purpose, peace, and prosperity for *every* single living being on the planet. We just all got kind of lost and forgot the most important things that really matter, like love, unity, self-expression, co-creation, and our connection to nature.

Despite the constant pressures of society to suppress my natural instincts, I continued on my quest for knowledge, personal discovery and growth, truth and love. I did not follow most of the set plans the current Western societal belief systems were trying to condition and program me with. Instead, I slowly found my own rhythm and followed that. And I know, first and foremost, to embody what the Indian revolutionary Mahatma Gandhi conveyed *"Be the change you wish to see in the world"*. So, it has been essential to work through my issues, focus on my own personal circumstances, and peel away all my layers, one by one. I am currently still peeling.

My journey has often been a very lonely and bumpy path. Though I have been blessed to meet like-minded kindred spirits, and have experienced many mystical moments, it was initially through music and books that I found eye-opening ideas and inspiring information. I intuitively sensed the words of wisdom in certain works and felt the deeper meanings being transferred as I absorbed the information. It mostly felt like a remembering, such as a moment of déjà vu. As I have become more confident and trusting in my intuition, it has grown stronger. It is through this intuition that I can sense, most of the time, when I am hearing rubbish or truth.

From a young age, I was faced with many struggles that eventually helped open me up to my spirituality and my connection to Mother Earth and the divine Universe. My parents divorced when I was three. Soon after, both parents remarried, unfortunately to not very nice people (luckily, my mum's third husband is a very good man). Between the ages of six and sixteen, I was surrounded by alcoholism and money problems, as well as emotional, physical, and sexual abuse. At the age of twelve, my father chose my stepmother and religion over his children, and I never saw him again before his recent passing. Out of everything I faced as a child, my father abandoning me was the hardest thing to heal from. It made me feel worthless and unloved for many, many years.

However, I would not change any of it! My experiences helped to shape me into who I am today, and I love who I am. As Kahlil Gibran wrote in *The Prophet*, "Your pain is the breaking of the shell that encloses your understanding."[1]

It is through my suffering that I began to ask deeper questions and strive to break cycles—cycles of abuse, alcoholism, neglect, and abandonment. And I hold no blame or anger in my heart, though I carried a deep sadness and feelings of unworthiness for many of my adult years. I have forgiven my parents and stepparents, for they were only doing what had been taught to them and what society had moulded them into. Our current society does not provide a space for whole, functional, loving, and thorough parenting. It actually does the opposite.

Nevertheless, with an open heart I continued to strive for my individuality, for love, healing, and for truth. Since I was little, I had found great comfort and strength in music—all musical genres. Music created a space for me to just be me, and it assisted in processing and releasing emotions built up in my body. I heard words of love and unity from artists like Bob Marley, Louis Armstrong, Enya, and the Beatles that rang true to my heart and offered me hope. I heard words from bands like the Red Hot Chili Peppers, the Doors, the Rolling Stones, Radiohead, Pearl Jam, Coldplay and the Cranberries (to name a few) describing the same utopian world of universal peace, love, and true happiness that I had been dreaming about since an early age. I heard words of suffering and heartache that comforted me in my own despair and reminded me that I was not alone. And I heard words of revolution that spoke of the changes coming to the world.

And books . . . oh so many amazing books! In my teens, I was extremely interested in philosophy and read about many different schools of thought. I was drawn to several branches of philosophy, such as metaphysics (the study of existence), epistemology (the study of knowledge), aesthetics (the study of the Arts) and ethics (the study of morals). I read the inspiring words of great thinkers like Aristotle, Confucius, David Hume, Hegel, Henry David Thoreau, Ayn Rand, and Carl Jung, to name a few.

Feeling lost and alone in a world of duality and suffering, I found companionship and words of hope from the past. In my early twenties I read Henry David Thoreau's words, "Not till we are lost, in other words, not till we have lost the world, do we begin to find ourselves."[2]

I realized then that my feeling lost was the point of awareness I needed to start understanding who I really am—not just a human being, but as a being of spirit. I became further aware that there was more going on than my one narrow perspective: I could connect with the nonphysical part of me—my nonphysical spirit side. The pain that I held in my body was ultimately assisting in this process of unravelling and cracking open.

For most of my twenties and thirties, I was extremely interested in "New Age" books on spirituality, yoga, meditation, self-healing, psychology, and the mind-body-spirit connections. I devoured texts on Eastern religions, cosmic beings, and quantum physics and channeled material about the human experience from the perspective of higher dimensional beings. Most of the books I read would find me through synchronicities in my life. So many times, I would be deeply contemplating a subject and soon after meet a random stranger that would just happen to mention a book on the very same subject. Needless to say, I acquired the books as quickly as I could and was never disappointed. They were stepping stones on my personal path of spiritual maturity and awakening to my infinite divinity.

Throughout my exploration of the written word, I was inspired by how much of the material discussed and explored combined spirituality and science. I discovered ancient texts about energy bodies, the chakras, spiritual awakenings, dimensions of consciousness, and the ascension of Mother Earth, including all of those who elect to join her. The material I read stimulated a deep internal remembering for me and described the same kind of utopian society I had been dreaming about since I was little. So much of what I read reflected and confirmed my own personal philosophies on life, love, relationships. Personal philosophies such as follow my own intuition and heart's desires; always lead with love; every single living thing is divine; there exists a higher purpose or plan for everything; and we have forgotten many of our natural divine abilities.

Some of my favourite authors of books on the topics of spirituality and science include James Redfield, David Wilcock, Elisabeth Hatch, Eugene Fersen, Carl Jung, and Vladimir Megre. For books on other dimensions of consciousness, cosmic beings, and channeled material, I love works by Jane Roberts, David K. Miller, Lee Carrol, Ester Hicks, Helen Schucman, and Lee Harris. My favourite authors on themes of self-help and self-realization include Matt Kahn, Eckhart Tolle, Don Miguel Ruiz, Ayn Rand, Hermann Hesse, Henry David Thoreau, Ralph Smart, and Ram Dass.

In my twenties and thirties, I travelled around various parts of the world. After facing and overcoming some serious health issues with my thyroid in my early twenties, I was driven to answer the call of my burning desire to see the world directly. Some of my journeys were short trips, and others were extended excursions. Just travelling to new countries and being immersed in other cultures opened a doorway of education for me. It offered a space for learning from direct, first-hand experience. But mostly, it opened up a path of deep personal discovery of myself, my strengths, my weakness, and my passions. Travelling helped me gain a broader perspective of the world; it helped me realize that no matter how much money we have or where we live on this planet, at our core, we are all the same. We all start this journey off with the birth of our soul into the physical, and end it with a death of the fleshly body as our soul moves on to its next journey. We all bleed, feel pain, experience love, and have dreams, purposes, and intentions. We all contain the same basic elemental makeup, though we make different decisions on how to develop, use, and share what we have.

The next biggest step in my personal growth occurred when I became a mother at the age of twenty-nine. After almost marrying a man from India and preparing to move there, I found myself back in Canada, alone and pregnant. Although, once again I was doing things backwards, the birth of my daughter opened a doorway of true miracles and unconditional love. It also helped to activate and strengthen many of my natural psychic abilities. Becoming a mother further ignited my intuition, revealed my ability to work with energy, and strengthened my telepathic skills. My baby girl helped me fully accept my own divinity and drove me to peel away more of my layers, break cycles of abuse, and face the darkness deep within me.

Creating life, and then watching that little life grow day after day, was like watching a miracle unravel right before me. This little miracle, my daughter, helped me appreciate and pay attention to the present moment more than I ever had before. Things were so fleeting; every day she would change somehow. This made me pay close attention to all the little details, to all the little moments.

Being a mother is one of the hardest things I have ever done, but it is also one of the most remarkable experiences. I have learned to be more patient, to love and be loved unconditionally, to continually strive for learning and the betterment of myself. And let me not forget the acceptance and adaptability to change I have had to face in every moment of motherhood. Change is automatically part of being a human being. The quicker we can accept this, the sooner we can learn to flow with the constant transformation and alterations life throws at us.

Another transformation occurred in my early thirties, when I met my future husband at the grocery store. He was also a single parent, so we quickly became a blended family of six. Although blending families together can be extremely difficult, it offered me a whole new playing ground to practise and develop my natural abilities. It also brought up more layers I needed to peel away.

Throughout my thirties, I dedicated time to further develop and practise my natural intuitive abilities to work with energy. I explored and practised various aspects of natural healing, such as aromatherapy, massage, crystals, yoga, Ayurveda, homeopathy, sound healing, and various energy work techniques (at the same time, I homeschooled my daughter, earned a Bachelor of Fine Arts degree, and started my own business). I also received healing energy work for my physical and mental bodies from many deeply connected healers. For several years, I was part of a healing circle where a group of us would get together and all practise energy work on each other. It was an incredible and safe space to practise my natural intuitive healing abilities and receive direct feedback on the results. This process helped to strengthen my confidence and assisted in establishing a deeper relationship with my spirit guides, such as Archangel Michael, Jesus, and the Arcturians.

During this time, I discovered Wilhelm Reich and his scientific findings of the natural energy found in all living things. He called it *orgone* energy. Through his work, Reich created "orgone accumulators," which transmuted negative energies back into harmonious, positive energies. Besides many other incredible things he was doing, Reich was healing all sorts of ailments in the 1930s and up until his death in 1957. I was extremely interested his findings and how, in the 1960s, people all over the world began recreating these devices based off of Reich's science. Still, today, many use these devices to transmute negative energies—such as EMFs and radiation—from computers, cell phones, cell towers, powerlines, and other electronic technologies. I am extremely sensitive to these energies, myself, and when I got my first orgone device, it brought me immense relief. So much relief, in fact, that I had to share it with the world. And so, in 2016, I started making them myself. I wanted to add an artistic flair to them. They could become things a person could wear, carry, display, or hang on a wall. For many years, I have sold them at fairs and markets, meeting thousands of beautiful souls in the process. It was at these events that I also facilitated healings, channelings, and powerful energy work, assisted by my higher self, my spirit guides and my hand-made orgone devices.

Then, another opportunity for healing and spiritual growth presented itself. For several years in my mid-thirties, various synchronicities in my life slowly led my husband and me toward the path of sacred plant medicines. Through an acquaintance, we were connected with a shaman who was facilitating local ayahuasca ceremonies.

After a few ceremonies, we were invited to a healing retreat in Peru run by our shaman's master teacher. For two weeks, we lived in the jungle, sat in on nine ceremonies, and participated in various other healing techniques. We radically opened then, exploring and reconnecting to ourselves, the divine Universe, and everything else in between. This experience could make up a completely separate book in and of itself. So much was revealed, removed, remedied, explored, shared, seen, felt, sucked out, and shoved back in. I was taken to what I called "the death pits," where I was immersed in the deepest suffering and darkness of my soul for what felt like an eternity. Once I journeyed through that, with the support of several shamans and my husband, I found my way to the light of my soul. I found wholeness and unconditional love, and saw glimpses of the spirit realms.

I have heard people say that participating in an ayahuasca ceremony can be like doing five years of psychotherapy in one night. The deep journeys of my ayahuasca ceremonies took me into other dimensions of consciousness and activated an extreme opening. I felt parts of my social conditioning unravel inside me. It also initiated an intense healing from traumas in this life as well as past lives.

After a few years of working with these South American sacred plants, I needed several more years to integrate everything that had happened to me physically, mentally, emotionally, and spiritually. Much of what I had identified with was no longer there or relevant. The ceremonies had healed, strengthened, and cleaned out my physical body, rewired parts of my brain, and cleared me of emotional baggage I had carried since childhood. I truly felt a deeper connection to nature, and the divine Universe blossomed inside every cell in my body.

Then, in 2020, I turned forty and the human population continued to go a little crazy. The entire globe was in "lockdown", and entered a space of isolation and forced stillness. For me, this went along with what I was already in the process of doing: hibernating and facing my own "dark night of the soul." I find it very helpful, now more than ever before, to embrace the flow of change and make plenty of time for self-care.

Now that you have a little bit of information about the journey of my spiritual growth thus far—and what led me to the subjects of personal development and the awakening of the planet—let us explore some key terms that will be touched upon in this book.

These are vast subjects, where many perspectives and interpretations are available. I am not an expert on quantum physics or on the religions of the world, though I am familiar with both. I can only speak from *my* gathered knowledge, life experiences, intuition, and perspective.

THE EGO

As a part of the human experience, we all have an ego. Our egos protect us in times of danger by telling us what to do or how to react to survive. Our egos remind us to put on clothes before going out of the house. The ego is essential to surviving the dualistic experience of the 3rd dimensional state of unconsciousness and consciousness.

In 1923, Sigmund Freud introduced the world to the concept of a psychoanalytic theory in his published paper *The Ego and the Id*. His theory is based around three components of the human psyche he termed the id, the ego, and the superego. The id consists of the instinctual and primitive aspects of the human mind, the superego is our moral compass, and the ego is the mediator between the desires, memories, opinions, and beliefs of the id and the superego.

Along with Freud, Carl Jung also shared great interest in the understanding of the collective unconscious aspects of the human psyche. They initially worked together before going their separate ways. I personally connected more with Carl Jung's approach and his theories on the personal and collective unconscious. And how, through our ancestral memories, we play out different archetypes we identify with during our lifetime.

Since the birth of these concepts involving the ego, much has been written and studied. The common thread of thought is that the ego revolves around our perceived separation from internal and external things, like feelings, possessions or people. The ego has an insensible and unconscious state of identification with desires and future outcomes. As Eckhart Tolle describes it, the ego is "a false self, created by unconscious identification with the mind."[3]

The ego, a part of us, has forgotten its true purpose and connection to all. This is causing us to become more focused on the desires of the unconscious mind, leaving out most of our heart consciousness. The ego believes it is not complete or whole and is extremely vulnerable and filled with self-doubt. It thinks, "If only I could be fixed, have more material possessions, or be someone or somewhere else." Even if these endless pursuits are finally fulfilled, the ego will still feel empty, worthless, and unsatisfied.

Most of the parts of ourselves that we identify with and think of in "I" terms are our ego and not the core soul level of our existence. The ego is an aspect of the human experience that involves a body, a soul, and an ego.

The ego part of our being identifies with:

- Our physical characteristics
- The things we own
- Our social status
- Our race and heritage
- How we think others perceive us
- The work we do

- The level of our education and knowledge
- The past and the future
- Our belief systems
- Our political beliefs
- Our sex and sexual orientation

At present, many people are experiencing an unravelling of their ego, layer by layer. It is time for the "death of the ego," which is actually a rebirth often filled with pain, regret, and discomfort. But once the ego surrenders to the process of changing from an unconscious state of mind to a state of conscious heart space, an opportunity will open up for the ego to fully integrate back into our divine self. This process of unravelling and integrating plays a big part in the collective awakening and the ascension. What we want to fix in the outside world actually needs to be first fixed on the inside.

But how do we help our ego fully surrender and be reborn in the awakened soul? That process is a phase in our spiritual evolution, where we all independently need to turn within and take an extremely close look at ourselves. We need to do an examination of our choices, habits, patterns, actions, reactions, and everything with which we identify. If there is a deep desire for an inner shift in consciousness, we need to seek our very own personal path for spiritual growth. That path will look very different for each individual.

The next step, after examining ourselves and our egos closely, is to make some healthy changes in our lives. Many of these changes will be extremely difficult and make us uncomfortable. But the results could lead us further along our path of spiritual maturity and awakening to our own divine consciousness. Maybe one of those changes could be to, first, develop an awareness of the self-judgments or judgments of others you have, and then shift your attention to a mantra of love or acceptance. Another change could be to stop trying to be somewhere or someone else. Try to accept who you are in this moment as well as all the circumstances you find yourself in. Shift your perspective on how you think about yourself, other people, your job, your partners, your home, etc. We even need to shift the perspective we have of the ego itself.

Although many people tend to view the ego in a negative context, it is an essential aspect of the human experience. Our ego protects us in times of danger or uncertainty and helps us attain and maintain our individuality. We need to remember that the ego is not our enemy, but rather a vital aspect of ourselves. It serves no purpose to either resist or go along with the desires of the ego. The ego is vulnerable and insecure, and in order to make a shift toward integration, the ego needs to be accepted, loved, supported, and sincerely heard. We hold space and do not act on the ego's desires, but we accept, love, support, hear, and make space for what the ego wants to express. No matter how uncomfortable it will be, let the ego have your full, undivided attention without any judgments, reactions, or arrangements to fulfill its desires. Just be very present with this part of yourself and see it from different angles and perspectives.

THE HIGHER SELF

Each and every one of us has a higher self that exists on a higher multidimensional plane of existence. The concept of the higher self is often associated with numerous religions and belief systems, but is also recognized in nonreligious circles of thought.

The higher self generally refers to the true nature of a human being. It is the aspect of our self that is completely balanced, eternal, and omniscient. It communicates to us through our intuition, dreams, imagination, gentle thoughts, and ideas. Since our connection to the higher self—for most of us—is very weak, communication tends to be like whispers in the wind. The clearer the mind is of stuff (thoughts, judgments, opinions, ideas, beliefs, etc.), the easier it is to hear the delicate whispers from the higher self.

From our higher self comes our intuition and the deep feelings and emotions from within us. It is our eternal connection to the multidimensional aspects of ourselves and the different planes of existence. The higher self resides in multidimensional planes of existence and from there, perceives its 3rd dimensional human self from a broader, all-encompassing viewpoint. This viewpoint is always from a space of unconditional love, compassion, and support. Never from a negative judgmental outlook, or with the desire to give up and abandon us. The higher self is ever-focused, ever-ready, and ever-present to love, support, and accompany its 3rd dimensional human self.

Through the spiritual awakening process, we are increasing the connection and the awareness to our higher self. The link grows stronger with the pursuit of our own personal betterment and the unravelling and integration of the ego. It is through a change in perspective, not location, that the higher self is revealed. It becomes apparent that the higher self was there all along, just not yet fully perceived.

With any level in strength of the connection to one's higher self, a great companionship is possible. The guidance of your higher self—your omniscient self—may assist in various aspects of your human life experience. The broader perspective of your higher self can help with situations such as how to face difficult circumstances, make hard decisions, and deal with loss or pain from a space of love and acceptance. Having a deeper intuitive guide that knows you so intimately may offer relief and direction in those lonely and uncertain moments of time.

So, how do we start connecting to our higher selves? We ask for help!

CONNECTING TO YOUR HIGHER SELF:

- Find a quiet place where you can be alone for a few minutes
- Take some deep breaths
- Relax your body and calm your mind
- Either out loud or in your head, say something like:

- *"Of my own free will, I call upon my higher self. Be with me now and always. May everything I say, do, experience, love, think, imagine, or create be guided by your all-knowing connection to the divine Universe from which we were made. And so it is."*

- Or *"My dear higher self—beautiful aspect of my eternal being—it is my intention that our connection grows deeper and stronger with every breath that I take. Love and create through me; speak and act through me. Help me to always lead with love. And so it is."*

- Or create a personal statement of your intention to connect with your higher self

• Take some more deep breaths and just bask in the space of intention and connection

• Be open, but have no expectations of the outcome. The connection may be very subtle. It may be so familiar that it's hard to even notice a difference. Let it be whatever it will be. There are no judgments or rigid beliefs here—only faith

• Now that you have made a conscious connection to your higher self, just be in this space and see what happens—quietly open and attentive—or ask for guidance, support or specific questions

• Thank your higher self

Later, when the connection becomes stronger, you will be able to establish the link to your higher self quickly, effortlessly, anywhere, and anytime. Eventually, the link between your 3rd dimensional human self and your higher self will fully converge and reunite in the 5th dimensional plane of consciousness. For now, though, we slowly develop and re-establish this divine relationship and become re-accustomed to the natural flow of co-creation.

THE CHAKRAS

In Sanskrit, the word "chakra" accurately means "disk" or "wheel." In essence, the chakras are powerful wheels of energy that exist in key positions inside and around the physical body. The chakras affect our physical, mental, and emotional well-being and play an important role in the flow of divine life-force energy throughout all our bodies. As Anodea Judith explains in her book, *Wheels of Life*, "Chakras are organizing centers for the reception, assimilation, and transmission of life energies."[4]

There are seven main chakras that go along the spine of the human body, starting at the base of the spine and leading up to the crown of the skull. These seven chakras match up with major organs and certain bundles of nerves found in the human body. Although the majority of information to be found on the chakra system only touches on seven of them, some schools of thought believe there are 144 chakras in and around the body. These chakras include: the soul star chakra (just above the crown chakra), the earth star chakra (located below the feet), and one chakra in each palm of the hands.

Chakras are spinning circular energy intersections that help us integrate and connect:

- The mind, body, spirit
- Spirit (nonphysical) and matter (physical), also known as Heaven and Earth
- All levels of the dimensions of consciousness
- Past and future
- Masculine and feminine

Throughout the realms of our subconscious and conscious awareness, the chakras provide a system where we connect and integrate the knowledge from one side of this awareness to the other and then back again. Our chakra centres are where we actualize and materialize our desires, dreams, and creative ideas, bringing through the nonphysical aspects of ourselves into the physical. They are where we find our motivation, our strength, our voice, and our ability to receive and give love.

So, where did the concept of the chakra system originate? In the ancient traditions of India, chakras are first mentioned in written form in the *Atharva Veda*. The *Atharva Veda* is Hindu scripture written between 1000-900 BCE (around 3,000 years ago). The complete work is compiled in twenty books containing around six thousand mantras. This ancient scripture is known for its everyday processes to create and live an abundant and fulfilled life. All that being said, the chakra system is also linked to the oral traditions of the Aryans from over 4,000 years ago. Both of these ancient cultures speak of the chakra system, which stems from yoga.

Yoga first came to the West in the 1890s, when an Indian monk named Swami Vivekananda visited the USA. He translated many books on the practice of yoga from Sanskrit to English and provided public demonstrations of the practice himself. Through this introduction to the practice of yoga, the concept of the chakras was also revealed to the Western world. These new concepts became very popular in the West, quickly spread, and offered Western society an alternative way of connecting with their body, mind, and spirit.

Understanding and knowing a little bit about these energy centres offers us practices and insights that we can implement in our lives to further our spiritual growth. Further, it increases our connection to, and knowledge of, ourselves, others, and the divine Universe.

A BRIEF DESCRIPTION OF THE SEVEN CHAKRAS:

1st Chakra – *THE ROOT*

Sanskrit name: Muladhara

Colour: Red

Element: Earth

Seed sound: LAM

Yoga poses (asana): Bridge pose, Tree pose, Mountain pose and Warrior pose

The root chakra is located at the base of the spine. It reflects our foundation and is where our stability, power, security, and survival instincts reside. As well, the root chakra assists in grounding the soul into the physical body, and the physical body into the Mother Earth. Whenever we are facing challenges or dangers, it is from the root chakra we draw strength.

2nd Chakra – *THE SACRAL CHAKRA*

Sanskrit name: Svadhisthana

Colour: Orange

Element: Water

Seed sound: VAM

Yoga poses (asana): Bridge pose and Goddess pose

The sacral chakra is located just below the belly button in the lower abdomen. This is where we find our creative and sexual energy, along with our passion and desire. The sacral chakra is home to your emotions. It is the space where we discover how to connect with our own emotions and the emotions of others.

3rd Chakra – *THE SOLAR PLEXUS*

Sanskrit name: Manipura

Colour: Yellow

Element: Fire

Seed sound: RAM

Yoga poses (asana): Boat pose, Bow pose, Pike pose and Woodchopper

The solar plexus chakra is located in the stomach area from your navel to the solar plexus. This is where our will power, confidence, self-esteem, and assertiveness come from. The solar plexus chakra contains our inner fire that drives the consciousness into action. It inspires a transformation from the unconsciousness within us to consciousness.

4th Chakra – *THE HEART CHAKRA*

Sanskrit name: Anahata

Colour: Green

Element: Air

Seed sound: YAM

Yoga poses (asana): Camel pose, Cobra pose and Fish pose

The heart chakra is located near the heart of the physical body. This is where we find our ability to give and receive love and to have empathetic compassion and connection with ourselves and others. The heart chakra is the middle chakra within the body and is considered the space of connection and integration from the lower and higher chakras. Being at the centre of our chakra system, the heart chakra brings recognition of the need for balance in all aspects of our lives: balance between our inner and outer realities, our mind and body, and our ability to give and receive love. There is a spaciousness in this middle point.

5th Chakra – *THE THROAT CHAKRA*

Sanskrit name: Visuddha

Colour: Blue

Element: Sound

Seed sound: HAM

Yoga poses (asana): Fish pose and Plough pose

The throat chakra is located near the throat. This is where we find and develop our ability to communicate, and express ourselves through sound and creativity. Then, we share this personal sound and creativity with humanity, nature, and the divine Universe. It is also where we attain the ability to truly listen and pay attention to others. The throat chakra is a gateway towards unity—unity within ourselves, with others, and the divine Universe.

6th Chakra – *THE THIRD EYE CHAKRA*

Sanskrit name: Ajna

Colour: Indigo

Element: Light

Seed sound: OM

Yoga poses (asana): Forward Fold pose, Child pose, Lotus pose and Downward Dog

The third eye chakra is located on the forehead between the eyebrows. This is where our imagination and dreams are seen and then manifested into the physical realm. The third eye chakra contains our psychic sight, which sees beyond the physical. It is a gift of sight—a connection point of our inner sight and our outer sight. In this space, we make internal interpretations of the physical and the non-physical worlds we exist in simultaneously.

7th Chakra – *THE CROWN CHAKRA*

Sanskrit name: Sahasrara

Colour: Violet to white

Element: Thought

Seed sound: No sound – *Silence*

Yoga poses (asana): Corpse pose, Lotus pose, Crocodile pose and Tree pose

The crown chakra is located at the top of the head. This is where we connect with our higher self, the collective, higher dimensions of consciousness, and the divine Universe. The crown chakra connects us with the cosmic consciousness—a space where the unconscious and conscious merge into a complete union. This union brings with it a state of profound full awareness and omniscience. From the crown chakra, we find a space from which we have the opportunity to achieve a fully awakened state of consciousness—timeless and space-less.

FINAL THOUGHTS...

From these chakras centres, we connect with and harness our divine universal powers. To function at their best, these energy centres need to be fully activated and spinning at their own optimal speed and rotation. This is a part of our spiritual awakening and the process of becoming our true divine nature.

I strongly recommend researching and learning more about these powerful and significant energy centres in the body. There are countless reliable sources that are available to gain a basic understanding of the chakras. Each chakra is associated with parts of the body, emotions, desires, colours, sounds, crystals, spirit guides, planets, elements, and so much more. Specific mantras and natural remedies are associated with each chakra to help promote optimal function and activation.

There are various types of people working with universal life-force energies to heal their clients from physical and nonphysical ailments. In most energy work, the work is actually being done with the chakra system of the body (see *Chapter 8—Healing Modalities* for a list of various techniques). If you haven't embarked on this journey yet, it might be helpful to learn more about the chakra system and implement some of the knowledge into your daily life.

DIMENSIONS OF CONSCIOUSNESS

Trying to understand the spiritual dimensions of consciousness is difficult for the 3D materialistic mind to grasp or convey. When exploring the nonphysical world (where words are obsolete), the path is not scientific or even provable. It is spiritual, and ultimately, it has to be directly experienced.

Originally, the word "dimensions" was used in theoretical physics in the mid-1800s and later in the beginning of the 1900s in quantum physics. The term was quickly picked up by science fiction writers and later, by the New Age movement. It has now become a familiar word to many people, though its meaning remains unclear when mentioned in the spiritual context.

There are many different schools of thought on the term "dimensions," both in the scientific world and the spiritual realms. To understand the spiritual aspects, it helps to, first, think of the dimensions from a physics perspective. First, there is a point, which has no dimensions; then, there is a line, which has one dimension. Next, a solid object has three dimensions, and then, there is the concept of the 4th dimensional space-time. When thinking in terms of the dimensions of consciousness, they are similar to mathematical dimensions, but they lack the spiritual aspect. Where mathematical dimensions deal with the physical world, dimensions of consciousness deal with the nonphysical aspects of our spiritual being-ness.

THE FIVE DIMENSIONS OF CONSCIOUSNESS:

1st Dimension: (unconscious)

    The cellular level of our being and our genetic codes

2nd Dimension: (unconscious)

    Our biological matter and automatic systems of the body

3rd Dimension: (conscious)

    Our physical body and ego consciousness

4th Dimension: (unconscious)

    Our astral bodies and higher human consciousness

5th Dimension: (super-conscious)

    Our light body and unity consciousness

There exist even more dimensions of consciousness beyond our current ability to imagine or perceive, but we are, at this moment in time, having a human experience in the 3rd dimension of consciousness, and therefore, our main focus should be on what is closest to us. Additionally, five dimensions of consciousness sure seem like enough to experience many lifetimes over. That is, until we have mastered what we wanted to master and then, we move on.

The levels of dimensions of consciousness can be compared with grade levels in school. All grades are important; they build on each other, and they offer opportunity for learning and growth. No one grade is more important than another. In both grade levels and dimensions of consciousness, we have the opportunity to evolve emotionally, mentally, physically, and spiritually.

Another incredible thing is that we are multidimensional beings. We exist in multiple dimensions at the same time. In one second of time, we are experiencing (though not always aware of it) many dimensions of consciousness simultaneously. In that second, we exist on the cellular level (1D), on an automatic biological level (2D), in the physical body (3D), and on the higher human consciousness level (4D). And, of course, many, many more dimensions are unknown to us at this time. We may not be aware of everything happening inside and all around us, but this is actually okay. This is part of being a human being. As we are evolving spiritually, our conscious awareness is also elevating to higher dimensions of consciousness. We are experiencing a collective awakening.

COLLECTIVE AWAKENING

At this time on Earth, a majority of human beings are in the process of a spiritual awakening, a collective awakening. Many are re-discovering their connection to everything, as well as their psychic abilities and their eternal divinity. Our planet is at a profound junction in time and space—we have entered the Age of Aquarius. Along with this, our planet is receiving an immense amount of cosmic energy, which is raising the vibrations of all living beings, as well as the planet itself. All of this is creating an opportunity for a collective awakening, a spiritual enlightenment of the masses. It is a time for a collective transformation.

Anyone who chooses, with their own free will, to evolve and take a step toward their soul's progress, has a part in the collective awakening. In the past, it took many, many years of deep meditation, isolation, and fasting to attain a spiritual awakening. But with the profound high vibrational cosmic energy pulsing throughout our galaxy, an opportunity is being created for a massive awakening to occur. Many are ready to stop following outdated egoic social systems that are not truly benefiting anyone, especially Mother Earth. It is time for the un-awakened programmed mind to reclaim its independence and remember its true purpose of co-creating with the divine Universe.

So, what is the collective awakening? First, it would help to consider what a spiritual awakening means for just one human being. We have two great examples to contemplate: Jesus of Nazareth and Gautama Buddha. From their humble beginnings, both of these men achieved a spiritual transformation and a rediscovery of their natural state of wholeness. With unprecedented spiritual openness, they both transcended time and space and regained their complete connection to the divine Universe. They rose above the duality and separation of the 3rd dimension, and became aware of the 5th dimension: unity consciousness.

Based on these two popular examples, a spiritual awakening is an inner shift in consciousness that causes a reconnection to our eternal divinity. Through the evolution and expansion of our soul, we regain full awareness of our omniscient self and our connection to everything. We fully unravel and integrate the ego mind with the soul and the body to form what is known as the light body. This enables us to exist, beyond space and time, in both the physical and nonphysical planes of reality. It also activates our divine powers and our psychic abilities.

On the planet right now, there are massive numbers of people on the path toward their own spiritual awakening, not just a small group. The ones already on this deep spiritual transformation are inspiring others to do the same. As a result, more and more people are expanding their soul's progress toward unity consciousness. This is a collective awakening—when a massive number of human beings are simultaneously awakening to their eternal divinity.

In the present day, many feel a profound lack of connection to themselves, others, and even nature. Rather than looking outside themselves, they are seeking spiritual growth in their own personal way. There are various synchronicities occurring in the lives of those who choose to see the shift in conscious awareness.

There is an increase in conscious awareness about:

- Our inner selves
- Our physical body
- Other life sharing this planet
- The physical world around us
- The nonphysical (spirit) world around us
- And *our ultimate connection to all of it*

Through this process of raising our conscious awareness, many are experiencing a shift in their perspectives on who we truly are and what we are capable of. The desire to focus on personal growth becomes more important than what others are or aren't doing. When we are ready to take a deeper, closer look at ourselves, the choices we make, and the actions we take, we are definitely on a path of spiritual awakening.

How do we achieve a spiritual awakening? First, we have to accept that we have absolutely no control over the process. We cannot control the things that happen, just how we respond to the situation. So, definitely get used to letting go: letting go of people, things, desires, ideas, beliefs, employment, etc. Find a way to flow with the ups and downs of life, instead of struggling against them.

After the process of letting go, it would be very helpful to de-program yourself from the social conditioning we have been subjected to since birth. Take a deep look at what you believe in and why. Look at the opinions you have of other cultures, the government, or natural medicines. Are they based on things we were taught and never considered for ourselves? Maybe we could distance ourselves from mainstream media, take a break from all technologies, and spend more time in nature. We could even just spend more time with ourselves and the thoughts, ideas, and opinions running through our heads.

Then there are our emotions! We desperately need to reconnect with our feelings and emotions: all of them, not just the good-feeling ones. Our emotions are deeply connected to our intuition and are like beacons of light directing us through our journey. The more open we are to our emotions, the stronger our intuition grows.

My last recommendation (though I will touch on more ideas to help throughout this book) is to fully embrace your healing journey. Take a deep dive into all that makes *you*, you. Look at all the aspects of your life, especially the ones you avoid or turn away from. What do you identify with? What positive and healthy changes can you implement in your daily life? What is it that is not serving you, but you continue to carry? What opinions and beliefs do you hold that do not originate from your own core personal philosophies?

Examine all the layers that make up who you are:

    For the mental body:

        Seek out the truth—your own truth

    For the emotional body:

        Accept all—you, others and the world

        Practise unconditional self-love

    For the physical body:

        Face your life-lessons—take action

        Overcome your fears and doubts

        Hold no judgments of yourself or others—show compassion

    For the spiritual body:

        Relate to the spirit (nonphysical) world

        Be open to your spirit

THE ASCENSION

The term "ascension" is usually associated with what happened after the death of Jesus of Nazareth, when he ascended to heaven. Nowadays, in nonreligious spiritual circles of thought, the ascension refers to Mother Earth—and those upon her that chose to—ascending into the 5th dimension of unity consciousness. This is similar to what happened to Jesus, except that we won't have to die to make this transition. Instead, we will reach a state of spiritual maturity and full awaken into our light body.

As discussed previously, the collective awakening underway on the planet is reconnecting humanity to its divinity. This part of ourselves, this divinity, exists in the 5th dimension of consciousness. The collective awakening has an important part to play in the ascension. The awakening is an aspect of the preparation of the vessel (our body and mind) for the miraculous shift.

There exists many possibilities of what will happen when the ascension occurs. It could be a gradual unravelling or a sudden shift. The ascension is not really possible for our current level of awareness to grasp fully. It is a subject of higher dimensions of consciousness beyond the reaches of the 3D human brain.

For those beings who choose to continue their path on the 3rd dimension of consciousness, there will be a timeline and space in reality for their journey through duality and separation. For those beings who choose to shift their consciousness toward unity and love, they will gain the connection, and the perception of the 5th dimensional plane of existence.

Now, that I have shared some knowledge on these elusive and eccentric subjects, let us dive in.

CHAPTER 1

THE HUMAN EXPERIENCE

AND

THE ASCENSION

Chapter 1
THE HUMAN EXPERIENCE AND THE ASCENSION

We are all on our very own special and unique spiritual journey. Many with the desire to learn and gain experiences, continue to evolve and expand their state of consciousness. Ultimately, and on many levels, we are all doing this together, as cosmically linked co-creating beings. Somewhere along the way, though, we forgot this or were led away from the knowledge of our divine origins and collective unity consciousness. For some time now, we have been living under the veil of illusion, which has been separating the physical realms from the spiritual realms—the physical from the nonphysical. This has caused us to perceive a world full of duality, suffering, and separation, leaving out the aspect of our true divine nature. This is a part of the current design for human experience on the planet, a design that binds us to the sole focus of this one life experience and inhibits our abilities to perceive all the multilayers and multidimensions of the divine Universe. But change is upon us and the veil of illusion grows thinner.

For many of us, we purposely chose to be here, now, for the massive shift in consciousness on this beautiful blue planet called Earth, or Mother Earth. Many are beginning to realize spiritual work does not need to be based on, or attached to, any one rigid belief system. Instead, spiritual work can be an inclusive path that takes ideologies from various perspectives on our creation, our purpose, and the Creator of it all (most commonly referred to as God). Current rigid, organized systems are naturally being replaced with a more direct personal experience with spirituality, a spiritual experience with one's own Self, the spirit realm, and the divine Universe. We are shedding our immature egoic states of consciousness and collective conditioned mental states. We are here to remember of our divine origins, and our complete unity with *everything*.

If these words are resonating with you, step completely out of the box with me...

Open your awareness to a bigger perspective, the perspective of your higher self and the divine Universe. Use one of your natural abilities, your imagination, to dive deeply into the subject of our origins. The ability to use the imagination and create images in the mind is a powerful step in the creation of the reality we see before us in the physical world.

Imagine for a moment . . . if each one of us is an omniscient, powerful, eternal speck of the divine Universe. We are connected to all of creation and have complete access to knowledge from every single experience ever had since the beginning of time. We could go anywhere in the Universe and take on any form we desired. Connected to the divine Universe, and to the most powerful energy in existence—love—we collectively co-created everything into existence. This magnificent co-creation unfolded over millions and billions of years, through the birth of other galaxies and planets that housed incredible life-forms.

During the process of creation, something happened; something changed. Along with co-creating rich, thoughtful, and exceptional creations of love, we also co-created the opposite. The divine Universe and love energy created us to become creators, ourselves, and experience everything. Unfortunately, this led us toward the creation of pain, suffering, separation, destruction, and fear. So, we destroyed relationships, environments, and even planets with this way of co-creating. We sank into an age of darkness. Slowly, we drifted away from unity, truth, and love and forgot our true connection to the divine Universe. Not everyone went down this path of darkness for long. Many returned to the light of unity and love. The divine Universe and love energy held space for our foreseeable return to the light and a time of positive co-creation that would eventually return for all.

For thousands of years now, many beings have been incarnating on this beautiful planet. Mother Earth provides a perfect place for souls, in human form, to rediscover our natural ability to co-create reality through a loving vibration of unity consciousness. We spend our lifetimes slowly unravelling our disconnection and disharmony, and maybe, just maybe, remember our true divine origins and the immortality of our souls. Part of our journey on this planet involves working through our past ancestral karma and helping others in need. Many of us came here to help usher in the dawning of the Age of Aquarius.

Continue on this out-of-the-box journey of imagination...

Imagine that we—eternal and sacred beings of light from higher dimensions of consciousness—requested, helped plan, and prepared for a journey into a human body in the 3rd dimension of consciousness, the dimension where our awareness and perspective was based on duality and separation. We went on a journey through the veil of time—the 4th dimension of consciousness—for a chance to co-create with love.

Imagine that our sacred souls were carried down by all our cosmic family into the miracle of the birth of a human being. We were given everything required and needed for the journey. Locked away in our DNA and cells are codes, memories, and psychic abilities that we may or may not unlock during this human lifetime on Mother Earth. With the veil of illusion and forgetfulness pulled over our senses, we play out our chosen roles in each other's lives and perhaps we start to awaken and activate our hidden codes and forgotten abilities.

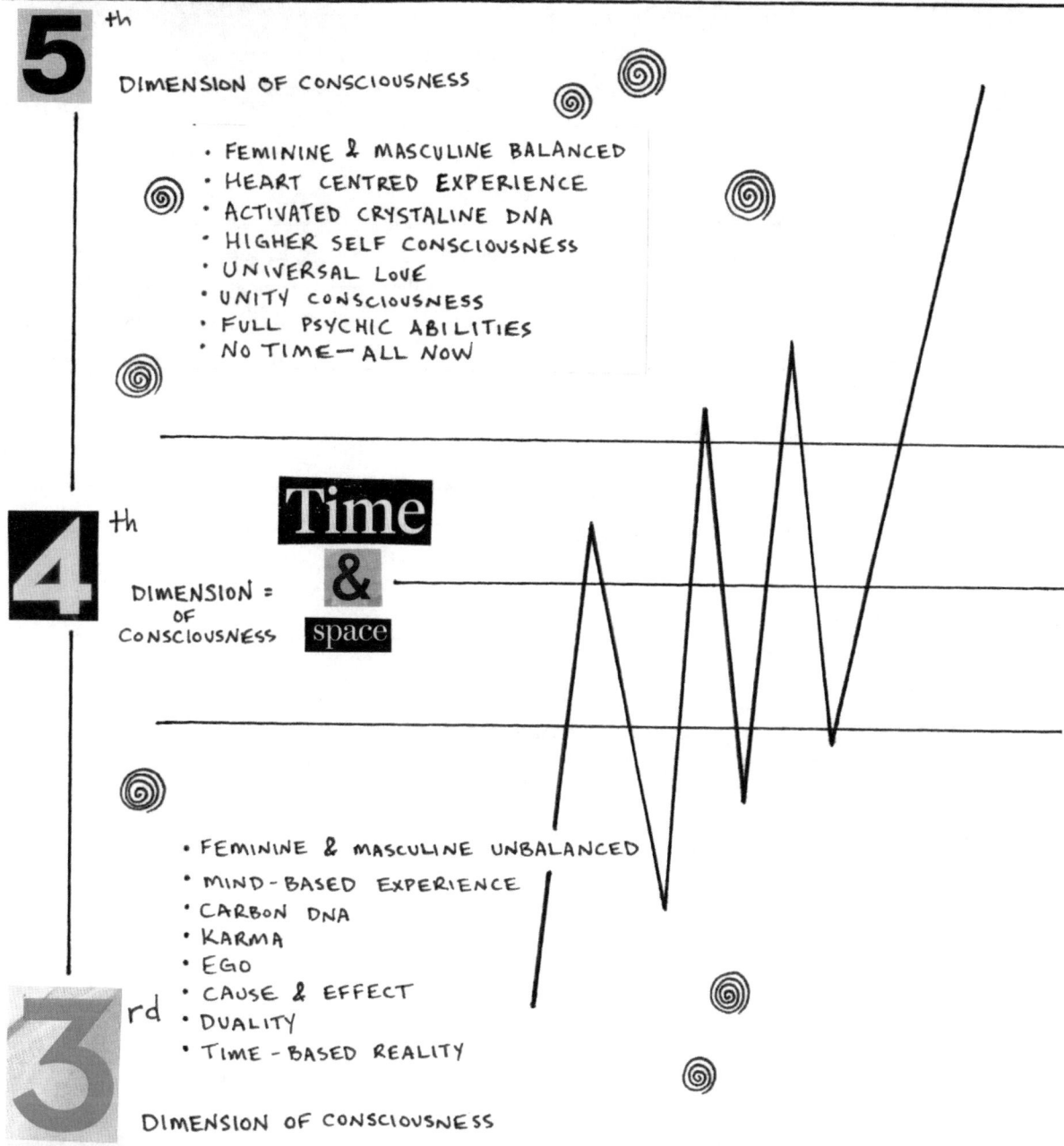

From LIGHT TO THE DARKNESS
...of the unknown

5th DIMENSION OF CONSCIOUSNESS

- FEMININE & MASCULINE BALANCED
- HEART CENTRED EXPERIENCE
- ACTIVATED CRYSTALINE DNA
- HIGHER SELF CONSCIOUSNESS
- UNIVERSAL LOVE
- UNITY CONSCIOUSNESS
- FULL PSYCHIC ABILITIES
- NO TIME — ALL NOW

4th DIMENSION OF CONSCIOUSNESS = Time & space

- FEMININE & MASCULINE UNBALANCED
- MIND-BASED EXPERIENCE
- CARBON DNA
- KARMA
- EGO
- CAUSE & EFFECT
- DUALITY
- TIME-BASED REALITY

3rd DIMENSION OF CONSCIOUSNESS

FROM DARKNESS TO THE LIGHT

> Well, guess what?
>
> *We are ever-expanding, immortal, sacred beings!*
> *We have lived many lives*
> *There truly is so much more than our five senses perceive*

At our soul level, we naturally vibrate from a state of pure *love*, and desire vast experiences. Here, we find ourselves in the struggle and beauty of the twenty-first century, in the dawn of the Age of Aquarius. It is a time of collective awakening, where we are elevating from a state of spiritual childhood toward a space of self-mastery. This is a space where we can expand our soul's growth, maturity, awareness, connection, and ability to co-create. For many lifetimes, we have been independently working on our own personal soul's growth. Now, we have the opportunity—with free will and choice—to expand and co-create from a space of unity consciousness.

In the beginning of this journey, we think we are the *victim* and need to be rescued. But, with our free will, we may slowly become more conscious, awakening our deep knowledge of who we really are—the *hero* of our journey.

> *Remember...*
> *We are the ones we have been waiting for*

> *We are the **light***
> *We are the **healers***
> *We are the **guardians***
> *We are the **love***
> *We are the **divine Universe***
> *We are the **saviours***
> *We are the **heroes***
> *We are the **magic***
> *We are **divine co-creation**...*
> *Ever-expanding infinite consciousness*

Our prominent gifts are our free will and our intuition. For the journeys planned out for our lifetime experiences, we established key attributes, but there is always free will. Set attributes would be like our gender, our physical traits, place of birth, the time period, our race, and possibly, big moments like falling in love, having children, or suffering injuries and illnesses.

With certain things planned to set the stage for our journeys, we still always have our free will. Things will happen around us and to us, but we ultimately choose what we do and how we will, either, <u>react</u> from the space of our ego or <u>respond</u> from the maturity of our soul.

Furthermore, to help set the stage of our journeys, and provide the needed characters, members of our soul family joined us on this experience. Our soul family comes with us from the higher dimensions of consciousness and through the veil of illusion to play key roles in our life. We come together to help achieve powerful healing processes, have advanced personal experiences in the human form, and learn from archetypal life lessons. All of this helps everyone involved evolve into higher states of consciousness—higher dimensions of consciousness.

Our soul family may take on important roles for us, such as our parents, husband/wife/partner, children, enemies, or adversaries. Imagine if the hardest roles played in our life—such as an abusive parent or our beloved unfaithful partner—were played by our closest soul family members. On a soul level, we chose to have these experiences and the ones who love us dearly across all time and space and are most familiar with us jumped at the chance to assist us on parts of our journey. Some parts that will be the most difficult and painful to experience.

We all play these roles for each other, down here in the duality of the 3rd dimension of consciousness. We may offer love and support, or we may test, offend and abuse each other—we *trigger* each other. We trigger a remembering.

What?! I ***chose*** to have these bad experiences?!

This comment may have *triggered the ego*

Take a deep breath . . .

You have done nothing wrong

Remember . . .
You chose these extremes in order to learn from them
You know you can survive anything
Out of the ashes, you will always rise
And rise again

Everything is exactly as it is meant to be
Why?
Because it is what is happening

Look at the grander picture
Look from the perspective of your ...

Eternal
Infinite
Divine soul
Always changing. Evolving. Growing.

This journey allows you to have a direct personal experience of everything ...
The good and the bad
Let go of everything you think you know
*Let go of everything you think you **should** know*
Forgive everything from the past—everyone, including yourself

◎ ◎ ◎

A GUIDE TO THE COLLECTIVE AWAKENING

From the Soul's perspective

There is no good or bad experience

There is only experience

Why would you want to have bad experiences?:

- To learn and gain wisdom

- To overcome difficulties for your soul's evolutionary purposes

- To further the completion of your galactic training—training many will use to come back and help others transcend to the 5th dimensional *heart space* of unity consciousness. In order to be able to help lift others from the deepest and darkest despair, it is useful and important for us to understand suffering on a first-hand basis. Having experienced body, spirit, and soul circumstances from all perspectives and with all senses will help us assist others through their personal 3rd dimensional journey

- To clear karma—past life karma or ancestral karma

Although bad experiences tend to make us uncomfortable, and trigger our emotions, they serve a higher purpose. Our bad experiences bring up the exact things we originally came down here to feel and heal on a personal and collective level and, hopefully, release and clear out.

Before we can have the future heaven on Earth, we must heal and clear out all the darkness from the past and the present. Many of us, called *light workers*, are here for various undertakings: for our own personal tasks, but also for a global, collective awakening and ascension. We are here to process and heal our own personal pain and suffering, as well as the pain from our ancestral lineages and Mother Earth. We do this simply by *feeling* the emotions, giving them our complete attention for as long as required, and offering authentic love. This cannot be achieved by turning away, distracting, numbing, or suppressing our emotions.

> **FEEL IT TO HEAL IT**

◎ ◎ ◎

It gets even more interesting, if we continue to imagine…

On top of our own personal tasks of soul evolution and maturity, we have come here to be incarnated on the planet at a very special and rare time. Throughout all the galaxies in the entire divine Universe, such an experience of an ascension, does not happen often. It is a huge and rare event. Our dear Mother Earth is ascending to the 5th dimension of consciousness, along with all living beings that desired this experience and opportunity. Another way to say it would be that we are on the threshold of the long-awaited Golden Age, and Mother Earth will become the garden of heaven.

> *Mother Earth, the garden of heaven?!*
> *It truly is all based on our perspectives:*
> *To some people, our planet right now is like heaven, whereas for others,*
> *it is hell.*
> *We are on the threshold of creating the garden of heaven for all sentient beings*
> *upon Mother Earth.*
> *We have chosen to come here at this very special time of . . .*
> ***Ascension***
> ***The Collective Awakening***
> ***Enlightenment***
> ***The Second Coming***
> ***The Golden Age***
> ***The remembrance of our divine origins***

This process of ascension has been happening for some time now. It is a slow process, when considering it from the perspective of our 3rd dimensional time and space. As infinite cosmic beings in training, what better way to learn how to assist others than to experience it all firsthand from direct personal involvement? The *body* has provided a space in which the *soul* can have this direct experience. The body is our companion to walk this journey with. Imagine, if you can, that our body is the one actually feeling, hearing, sensing, smelling, tasting, in pain, or in a state of joy. Meanwhile, the conscious part of our being, the place where thought and true wisdom exist, is the soul part of us. Deep inside, the soul just witnesses the experiences of the life being had and supports the body through it all—a constant companion. This design is set up so we can gain experience firsthand to aid us along this path of training, all while there are three experiences happening together at the same time—*the body, the ego and the soul.*

> The *body* is the one who needs to be healed
> And it is the *soul* that has the power to facilitate the healing
> The *ego* needs to be acknowledged, loved, fully heard, and not rushed
> Then all three experiences can fully integrate to form the *light body*

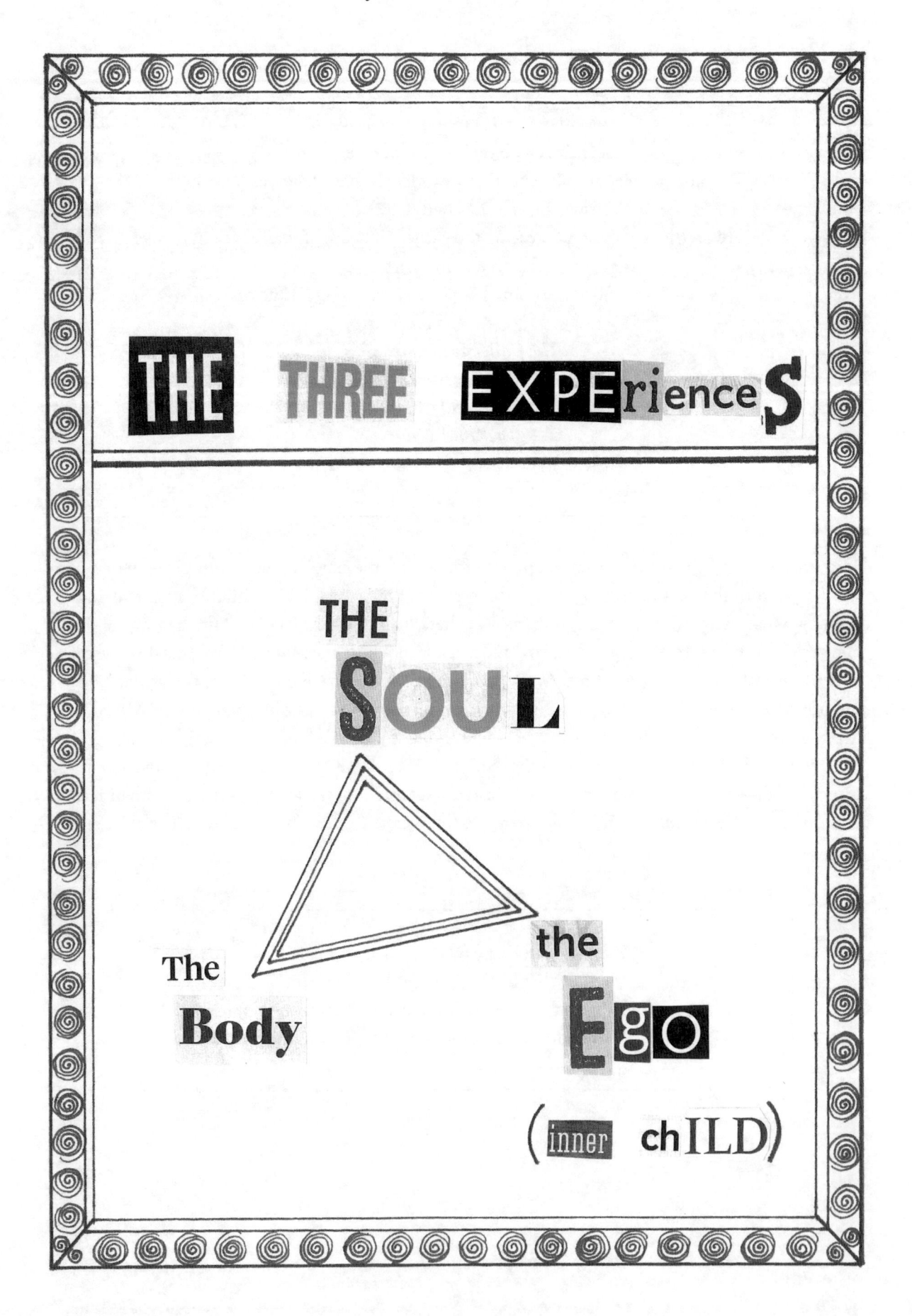

THE THREE EXPErienceS

THE SOUL

The Body   the Ego

(inner chILD)

Having a deep conscious awareness of the three separate—yet connected—experiences going on in this one form (the human body) can lead to a deeper relationship and understanding of many of our choices. Those choices include how to take care of ourselves better and how to create deeper connections to everything in this life.

With this great change in awareness—and with the awakening process underway—strong emotions come to the surface, as well as symptoms that affect our physical, emotional, and mental bodies. This process of change requires a lot of deep digging inside and looking at yourself from all angles, one layer at a time. Some of the layers can be joyful to peel back, while others can be extremely painful.

Many of the symptoms a lot of us are experiencing are also known as "ascension symptoms." They can be confusing, annoying, and unexplainable and then suddenly disappear one day, only to reappear another time. Through this book, I hope to offer some ideas to help you understand what is happening, as well as suggest things you can do to help yourself through this process. I will guide you on how to move, clear, and heal the energies raging through us at this time. And I will remind you: *You are not alone!*

I have compiled various tools, advice, and activities that have helped me along my journey of awakening. I truly hope it helps! May at least one thing I say bring your dear heart some relief!

This is a vast and ever-expanding process. We are beginning to experience a new spiritual paradigm. On a conscious and subconscious level, we are slowly becoming acclimatized to this new level of energy that it brings. We are experiencing brief periods of time in the 5th dimension of consciousness, filling our bodies with cosmic, divine, universal energies. We then return to the 3rd dimension of consciousness to give our bodies time to integrate and adjust. And so, we slowly yo-yo back and forth, expanding, stabilizing, and raising our vibrations until we reach the tipping point and *ascend*.

Let us remember to be easy on ourselves and others, to try to accept what is happening, and not to try to rush this process. Remember, this is the process we came here to experience, so let us experience it step by step and make the most of every bump and groove along the way. If we fail, fall, or totally miss the mark, *it is okay*—we get back up and try again.

CHAPTER 2

THE BODY AND ASCENSION SYMPTOMS

Chapter 2
THE BODY AND ASCENSION SYMPTOMS

The Earth itself, and many of the sentient beings upon this blue planet, are experiencing their own spiritual awakening. This individual, yet collective, awakening is preparing us for the ascension to 5th dimensional unity consciousness. There is an upgrade in energy and vibrations throughout our galaxy. It is affecting us on an emotional, mental, and physical level. Many of us are changing from carbon-based DNA into our *light bodies*. We are leaving the 3rd dimension of consciousness, based in duality, and ascending into the 5th dimension of universal *love* consciousness—beyond time and space (the 4th dimension).

The ascension process is elusive to us humans. This rare occurrence is not something that is easy to grasp with our current state of consciousness. Although, intuitively, we can sense that something is happening within and around us, we cannot physically prove or show these changes. These changes are mostly occurring inside us.

This process will take as long as is required to allow all involved beings to achieve their own individual awakening. As we are all unique, divine specs of *Source—the divine Universe*—so will each of our journeys be throughout these intense changes. That being said, I have noticed various symptoms that are quite common for anyone undergoing the awakening process and the ascension. In order to understand these symptoms, and where they are coming from, it helps to re-establish a deeper connection to our physical bodies.

Light Body

Rainbow Body

Awakened

Ascended

Enlightened

Christ Consciousness

ESTABLISHING A DEEPER CONNECTION:

Based on my personal experience with ascension symptoms over the past twenty years, it became very obvious that developing a deeper communication and connection with my body was important. After my personal realization of the three different experiences simultaneously occurring within me (the *body*, the *soul*, and the *ego*), I further realized the importance of respecting, honouring, and accepting each one of my individual experiences for their own part in my journey. Everything occurs for a higher cosmic purpose, a purpose that was mostly misunderstood or misinterpreted at the time.

We are, at the core, souls—eternal divine beings that have descended into the 3rd dimension of consciousness to experience and learn for our own evolutionary growth. Our mothers' bodies and properties of Mother Earth helped to create a physical form—the body—to encompass our celestial soul. The body provides a vessel in which to carry out our own independent and unique adventures on this planet. The ego is an internal, ever-present aspect of our earthly physical form. It is responsible for protecting the body physically, emotionally, and mentally. In our current society, however, the ego has run wild and unchecked and has almost taken over our main focus in all aspects of our lives and society as a whole. But, it is okay, this is part of the journey—to go down the path of ego and then to switch course back toward the path of our soul.

With this deeper understanding that *I am not my body, my body is my companion*, a deep shift in consciousness occurred. The body is primarily the one experiencing feelings, pain, hunger, cold, heat, etc. Therefore, I need to be in complete service to, and support the needs of, my body.

Unfortunately, most of the current population is solely focused on personal desires, which are really just the desires of the ego. We need to shift our focus toward universal desires, where we are mainly in service to the collective divine universal consciousness. This shift of focus, in turn, will bring us more fulfillment and connection than we could ever imagine.

> *We are not here for our own personal desires*
> *We are here to be of service to universal desires*
> *And the divine Universe desires the collective co-creation of love*

> **Personal Desires:**
> - Materialize from the ego
> - Are small and usually for self-interest
> - Come from a narrow perspective
> - Never fulfill or satisfy us
> - Drain our energy, our universal life force
> - Perpetuate the continuation of the karma cycle
>
> **Universal Desires:**
> - Materialize from the soul
> - Are vast and benefit the collective consciousness
> - Come from a broad perspective
> - Fulfill, include, and satisfy all
> - Fill us with energy, with universal life force
> - Open you up to possibilities beyond anything you could conceive of
> - Are where everything works together, in a state of flow
> - Fulfill and complete the cycle of karma

WAYS TO COMMUNICATE WITH THE BODY:

Ask the body questions . . .

    Is there something you want to share?

    How are you feeling?

    Is this my pain? Or the collective's? Or ancestral?

    What do you need?

    How might I serve you?

There may not be any reply. You might not hear, feel or sense anything at all. This is okay. Essentially, we have been ignoring our bodies for so long now, it may take time to re-establish the communication lines. But you will, if you keep asking and creating space to listen, really listen. Even if it is not something you want to hear, or it scares the hell out of you. Be easy on yourself. It will feel better once we face it, instead of looking away. There may already be current habits that you know are not right for your body . . . maybe now you are ready to listen and take sincere action.

Eventually, the lines of communication will open up. The answers may come as a thought, an impulse or a feeling. It might be very soft and subtle or insistent and strong. Give yourself time and space to open up to this unfamiliar connection. Most of us have not been listening to our bodies, or we haven't known that we should. We need time to remember, reconnect, and relearn how to have this deeper communication and ability to authentically listen.

When I first started to talk with my body, the connection was very subtle and soft-spoken. The more I continued to ask, and waited patiently for a response, the better the connection became. It evolved into a process of taking action and implementing my body's requests into my daily life. Some were big shifts and not very easy to make, while other changes came about with less resistance. It became apparent rather quickly that this new, deeper communication with my body, greatly assisted in moving and clearing out unwanted and stagnant energies.

> **Clearing Out:**
> - Old patterns
> - Old habits
> - Out-dated beliefs
> - Individual traumas
> - Personal karma
> - Ancestral traumas
> - Ancestral karmas
> - Mother Earth's traumas

Remember to keep it simple. Start with yes or no questions. Let your intuition and feelings guide you. Open yourself up, and quiet your mind. Take some time to really focus on the body. Bring into your awareness all parts of your body. Start with your feet and slowly work your awareness up to the top of your head. Try to feel the life-force energy pulsing through your body. Give your body some options like:

- Would you like to go for a walk in nature?
- Would you like to be still/rest/sleep?
- Would you like a healthy snack?
- Would you like some water? Herbal tea?
- Would you like to have a bath? Or shower?

Once I established a stronger open-line communication with my body (and I'm still working on it), I had an easier time knowing if what I felt (mentally, emotionally, or physically) was:

- Mine
- Ancestral

- The collective consciousness
- An ascension symptom
- A sickness or toxin clearing from my body

It is very important to remember, especially at this time, to take care of our bodies. We need to support, seek proper medical advice, and follow through with treatments. It is easiest to reflect back on symptoms experienced to determine whether or not it was an ascension symptom. Either way, the body requires proper support and care for all its mental, emotional, and physical needs. Whether it is the beginning, middle, or end of an issue, give your body the self-care it deserves. Approach your issues from all angles using natural remedies, as well as professional medical advice.

OUR HANDS FOR SUPPORT

I use my hands often to help my body when it is experiencing pain, discomfort, or ascension symptoms. We already do it instinctively, but are not even aware of it. For example, there are times when you are so frustrated you feel like your head is going to explode, and you bury your face in your hands. The energy centres in your hands are helping to move and clear out the energy gathered and blocked inside your head.

> ### *We have powerful chakras in our hands*
>
> In the palm of each hand, a chakra vibrates and spins. Chakras are powerful healing instruments and something you can use anywhere, anytime.
> Try the following . . .
> Place your hands wherever you feel discomfort, pain, pressure, or anxiety
> Take some deep breaths
> Set a few intentions for what you would like your hands to clear, lessen, release, and support
> Hold your hands there as long as you feel inclined to
> Send *love* and sentiments of support for these areas of the body

Along with a deeper connection with my body, it became easier to know if what I was feeling was an ascension symptom, if my body was clearing out toxins, or if I was empathizing with trauma from the collective consciousness. Ascension symptoms can be subtle or extremely intense. I have noticed with my ascension symptoms that they can materialize strongly and then pass quickly. They also tend to be stronger during daylight hours and then pass in the evenings, only to resurface in the wee hours of the morning. I also noticed that they tend to come and go, even if I have not changed anything in my habits or routine. I must also mention that I still consult with my family doctor and naturopath for advice and guidance on health issues. I am open to all types of healing modalities from all cultures of the world, though I mostly use natural techniques to treat my ailments.

For a period of time, I would have an ascension symptom of shocks or waves of energy shooting up my legs which would happen mostly at night (my kundalini energy awakening). I had a few months where I would get sudden, sharp pains in my neck and have visions of crowds of people watching me (clearing out of past life traumas). I have also had years now of ringing in my ears that come and go, and waves of exhaustion and sleepless nights. In response, I love, support, and communicate with my body through this process. I make changes in my lifestyle to offer more support and less resistance. I request the help and support of both my higher self and my spirit guides (in *Chapter 7*, I discuss spirit guides). I also seek the advice and services of a professional medical doctor, naturopath, or specialist. It is best to cover all the bases: the physical and mental areas, but also the spiritual areas.

So . . .

WHAT ARE SOME ASCENSION SYMPTOMS?

- Tiredness, extreme exhaustion
- Sleepless nights—sudden jolts of energy, awakening often and being very alert
- Vivid and intense dreams—waking up exhausted emotionally, mentally, and physically
- Foggy brain—cannot think clearly, memory loss, slow mental processing
- A spacey feeling
- Headaches
- Stomach issues—gas, bloating, diarrhea, pains
- Eyes very sensitive to light and movement
- Very sensitive ears
- Dizziness
- Feelings of depression—doom and gloom
- A feeling of nothingness and disorientation
- An "out-of-body" feeling

- Feeling easily overwhelmed or overstimulated
- Feeling like you are losing your mind or going insane
- Feelings of anxiety and panic
- Feeling like time is speeding up
- Feeling out of place or homesick—a deep longing to go home
- Sudden loss of friends, jobs, activities, habits, home, identity
- Energetic legs, restless legs, shocks of energy
- Very emotional and sensitive mental state
- Weird, unexplainable body pains that come and go (clearing energy blocks)
- Seeing or hearing things that others do not perceive
- No sense of *identity*—all labels, archetypes, roles fall away
- No motivation
- Very sensitive to other's energy
- Things that you loved and enjoyed in the past, no longer bring you relief or pleasure
- Weight gain or loss (with no change in habits)
- Hot flashes or feeling extremely cold

> *We are activating our crystalline DNA*
> *And being blasted with rays of energy*
> *Divine energy is raising our vibrations*
> *At times it can be very intense*
> *Just take it . . . one breath*
> *One moment*
> *One day*
> *At a time*
> *It will take as long as it takes—no more, no less*
> *This is the process we came here to be a part of*
> *A part of co-creating the divine Universe*

HOW TO SUPPORT THE BODY DURING ASCENSION SYMPTOMS:

- *Be ease on yourself!*
- Water—drink plenty of pure, alive water
    - No fluoride
    - Bathe, shower
    - Go in or near natural bodies of water
- Essential oils
- Crystals
- Eat lots of *real*, homemade food
- Avoid consuming high-refined sugar
- Lots of rest and sleep
- Meditation
- Gentle walks in nature
- Laughter
- Massage
- Yoga, gentle stretches—Move the body = Move the energy
- Be creative—doodle, draw, paint, sing, dance, bake, write, etc.
- Listen to calming 432hz or 528hz music
- Breathe
- Ask for help—from your family, friends, higher self, spirit guides
- Take supplements, vitamins, minerals, plant medicines
- Express your emotions—feel it to heal it
- Avoid the use of electronic devices
- Spend some time *alone*—pondering, integrating, daydreaming, processing, etc.

> *Everything on this planet is here to help you on your journey*

HOW LONG WILL ASCENSION SYMPTOMS LAST?

Unfortunately, there is no one answer. We are cosmically linked, but at the same time, we are all on our own unique paths. For some, the journey from ego to soul will take longer and be more difficult. Others will be more willing to let go and change. Some may suffer deeply at a young age, thus creating an opportunity to awaken sooner, as a result of their personal suffering.

Know that these symptoms will not last forever, but also remember this was the path you selected for yourself. You came here with the purpose of gaining first-hand experience, of learning, of remembering. You came here for the opportunity to grow and evolve your soul.

We will, of course, reach the end, but it is the *journey* we came here for. There is no need to rush through the very journey you have come here to experience.

> <u>BE PRESENT</u>
> *With your journey*
>
> <u>BE PRESENT</u>
> *With your experience*
>
> <u>BE PRESENT</u>
> *With yourself and others*
>
> <u>BE PRESENT</u>
> *With your feelings*
>
> <u>BE PRESENT</u>
> *With the present moment*

> The present the *divine Universe* has gifted you with…
> Is the human experience

This is a slow process of unravelling, of growing and evolving spiritually. We need to give this process respect and patience. We need to give ourselves and others respect and patience on…

The Journey
The Path
The Process
The Unfolding
The Remembering
The Awakening

> *Follow your intuition*
> *Listen to your body*
> *Stay in your heart-space*
> *Respect the mind*
> *Only use the mind when you need to*
> *Otherwise…*
> *Stay in your heart-space*
> *Know that things will always change*
> *There will be an end*
> *But you didn't come here for the end…*
> *You came for the journey*
> *For all the moments of the human experience*

My own personal journey of the awakening process has come in many different stages. In the beginning, it was subtle and gentle, filled with a desire for knowledge and an opportunity to follow my heart and aspirations. These aspirations did not reflect or fit in with the social norms modern society impressed upon me.

Since a young age, I was very open and eager to learn about other cultures, beliefs, ideas, history, art, metaphysics, cosmic beings, other planets, stars, astrology, the moon, philosophy, great thinkers from all cultures and eras, great artists, writers, health and wellness, alternative medicines, natural medicines, nature, Mother Earth, land, water, air, animals, other dimensions of consciousness, parallel universes, galaxies, psychic abilities, psychic phenomenon, karma, past lives, chakras, Eastern philosophies, ancient civilizations, and so much more.

For decades, I have spent countless hours poring over books, connecting with other like-minded people, and travelling around a bit of the world. After spending much of my time exploring the outer world and beyond, a shift occurred and I went inward, into self-exploration. I dived deeply into a personal exploration and reflection of my own beliefs, thoughts, choices, and desires. I took a deep look at my daily choices, the context of my inner voice, my addictions, the many faces and roles of my ego, how I tune things out or what I use as a crutch to distract me, what food choices I make, what I put in, on or around my body, and more.

The time I spent exploring and gaining knowledge . . . which of course, to a degree will always continue, has now become less important. My focus slowly changed direction inward and when that started to happen, I experienced a shift in the way I was spiritually advancing. It stopped being about what I needed to heal next, what I needed to learn next, what I needed to process next . . . though, in the background, those things will continue to unfold. It just was no longer the main focus for me.

During the beginning of this transition, ascension symptoms became a daily thing that were sometimes all-consuming and very intense. It became a necessity to really focus on myself and the needs of my body. It was also important to set boundaries, to limit the amount of technology I was exposed to, and to disconnect from mainstream society as much as possible. Much like hibernation, or going into a cocoon stage, I became a bit of a hermit or recluse.

If I ignored the symptoms or was too busy to deal with them, they would just come back again or intensify, so I would have to listen. I got good at listening and letting go of trying to do everything, please everyone and instead, started to trust that, really, everything is as it should be. When it is time to change, life will change, and I just need to change with it.

I'm not perfect. I am not done with my journey of awakening . . . I will never really be done with something that is always beginning, unfolding, and flowering. I am still integrating my ego. I still make mistakes. My biggest lesson for this lifetime is rediscovering my worthiness.

I am writing this at a time when I am still undergoing the ascension process and experiencing various symptoms. It is becoming less intense, or maybe I am getting better at handling them, so I bounce back and rise up faster.

It is not a short journey. It is not a path for the faint of heart. It is deep. It is intense, overwhelming, lonely, and all-consuming. It is also beautiful. Though it can seem endless at times, time can be relative to the situation and perspective. Something can be perceived by one person as endless, whereas for another, the same thing could be fleeting.

Let us embrace this journey of ascension—this global collective awakening of our planet—with an open heart and try not to rush through the process. It is the process that we came here to go through, including all the ugly, painful, overwhelming, beautiful, breathtaking, and lovely moments. We just have to keep going, keep getting back up and dusting ourselves off.

Every day you wake up is another chance at being the _you_ you want to be. It really is within our power and grasp to manifest a peaceful and loving planet for all. For now, though, I can choose whether or not to perfect my skills. I can decide whether or not to undertake some deep healing. I can choose to help someone or only myself. I can get into the _flow_ of the divine Universe more and focus less on the egoic game of unfulfilled personal desires.

It Is Okay To Let It All Go . . .

- Expectations
- Roles
- Desires
- Dreams
- People
- Places
- Opinions
- Thoughts

- Ideas
- Titles
- Goals
- Labels
- Rules
- Beliefs
- Stereotypes
- Knowledge

Let the whole character of who you are go
It is not the real you
You are so much more
You cannot get it wrong
It is all just lessons to learn
And experiences to be had
By the soul in the human form

CHAPTER 3

WATER

Chapter 3
WATER

> *Water* is essential to our planet
> *Water* makes up more than half of our human bodies
> *Water* is used for growing, preparing and cooking food
> *Water* is utilized for cleaning and purifying
> *Water* sustains life

WATER FOR DRINKING:

It is common knowledge that we need clean drinking water to sustain life. Our bodies are made up mostly of water. For babies, water makes up seventy-five percent of their little bodies!

Unfortunately, for many on this planet, adequate clean drinking water is scarce or even unavailable. Sadly, this is not just in developing countries.

Tap water has no life force left in it. The water has travelled through kilometers of pipes, robbing and disconnecting it from its source of life-force energy—nature. It is my belief, from gathered knowledge that there are people out there who are pumping our water with harmful things, such as fluoride. Why would they do that, you ask? They do it to calcify and block our pineal gland. The pineal gland is located near the 6th energy centre (chakra), our third eye, which enables us to see beyond the veil of illusion and connect with the multi-dimensional divine Universe of which we are a part of. The pineal gland is a source of great power, your psychic powers.

Through the power of science, people have discovered that the pineal gland contains DMT, which is a very powerful chemical in all living things that floods our bodies at the time of birth and death. It also has retinal muscles, just like your eyes, and these retinal muscles do not help us see our outer reality. Instead, they connect us to our *inner* reality and the universal collective consciousness.

WATER H_2O

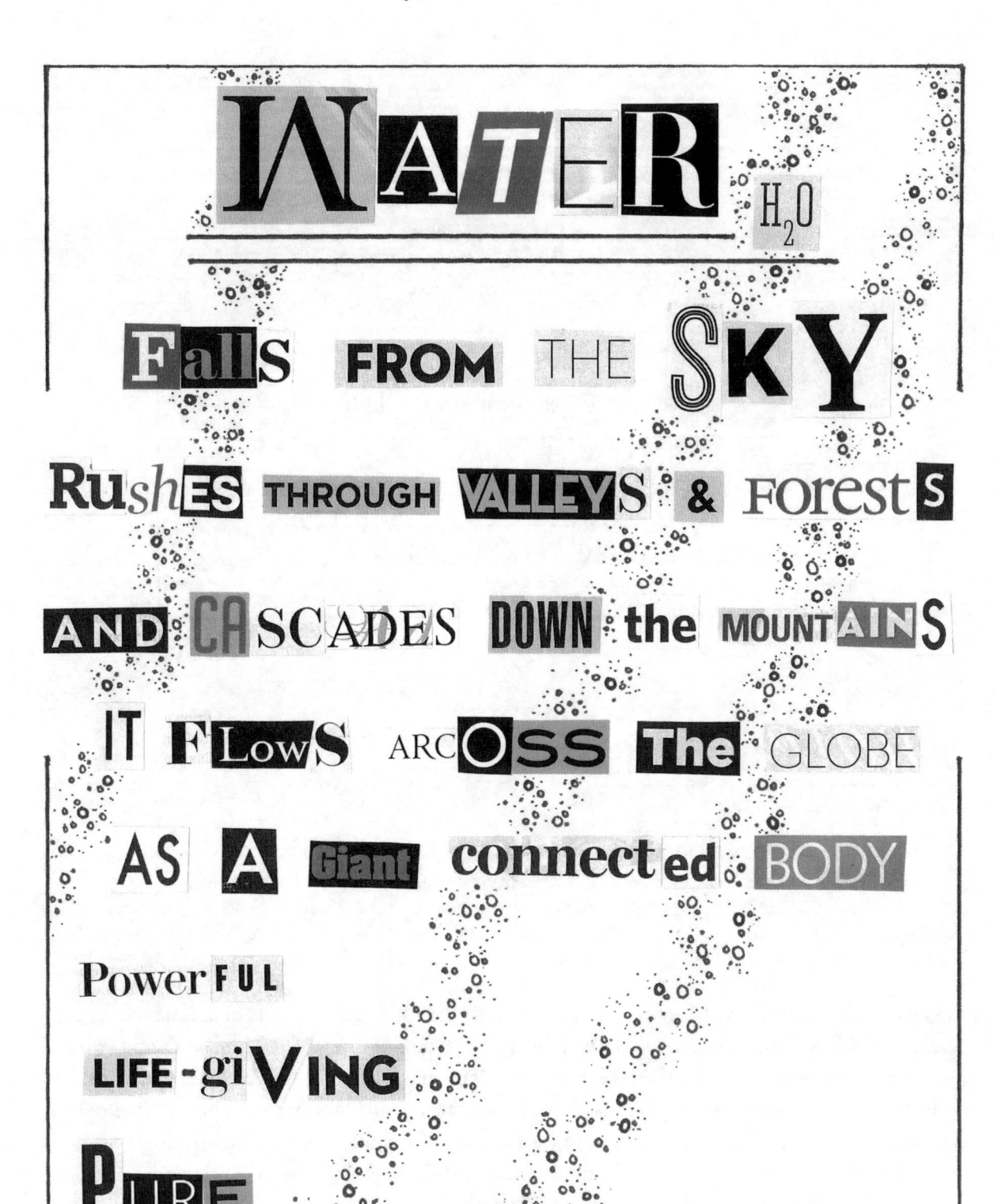

Falls from the sky

Rushes through valleys & forests

And cascades down the mountains

It flows across the globe

As a giant connected body

Powerful

Life-giving

Pure

A sacred miracle in form

Another huge problem is bottled water. Firstly, we are using oil to create plastic. Both products are extremely harmful to the planet, and sadly, better alternatives are being suppressed. Secondly, after the water is filtered, fluoride is added and then bottled in plastic. Here it stays until consumption, possibly being exposed to sunlight and heat, causing the plastic to breakdown. Where do the tiny molecules of plastic go? They go into the water and the person consuming it.

If you have to drink bottled water, look for spring water with *no fluoride*. I recommend staying away from anything that says "filtered water." Instead, purchase a high-quality reusable drinking bottle . . . not made from plastic. Use metal, glass, or copper. Copper dishware has been used for thousands of years in India, to serve and store food and water. There are many scientific studies that show the benefits of storing water in copper, as well as cooking and storing food in copper containers.

It is also very beneficial to acquire your own water-filtration system. There are various water-filtration systems available that offer a healthier way of getting good water for our bodies. I will warn you: They are expensive up front, but well worth every cent. In the long-run, it would be similar to buying bottled water for a couple of years, and really, can we put a price on our health? Feeling healthy, energetic, alive, and vital and having fewer health problems, better flushed systems, and a fully functioning brain are reasons enough to stay hydrated with clean, healthy, and life-infused drinking water.

My family purchased a Berky™ water-filtration system. It contains ceramic filters and fluoride filters in the top section, where we add tap water in to be filtered. In the container below, where it collects the freshly filtered water, we have special rocks to balance out the pH levels and add natural minerals back into the water. Below the whole thing, we have one of my hand-made orgone devices to add to the clearing and charging of life-force energy in the water.

So, how much water should we consume? Staying hydrated does not have to be a chore or something else to add to our "to-do list." By having more awareness of what we are already consuming and adding a bit more into parts of our routine, we can easily consume a sufficient amount of water in a day. Also, remember that certain beverages will actually dehydrate our bodies, such as soda drinks, coffee, black teas, sugary fruit juices, alcohol, and energy drinks.

> **Remember . . . we can get water from other sources like:**
> - Fruit
> - Vegetables
> - Smoothies
> - Herbal teas
> - Nut milks
> - Coconut water

WAYS TO ENJOY MORE WATER:

- Add a slice or squeeze of lemon juice to your drinking water

This adds a refreshing flavour to your water. Lemon is also very beneficial to our health. It is high in vitamin C and can balance our body's pH levels and make our bodies more alkaline. You can also try lime, or both together.

- Heat up water and make a pot of herbal tea

A variety of natural herbal teas are readily available in countless flavours. Many herbal teas have huge health benefits, both physically and emotionally. A hot cup of herbal tea can feel like a warm hug on a cold day; it can also sooth a dry, scratchy throat or help settle an upset stomach. It can calm or comfort you and help you relax into sleep. Plus, most herbal teas have no caffeine or sugar, so they hydrate the body.

- Get vitamins, fibre, and water by making smoothie popsicles

Make your own healthy smoothie with fruits, vegetables, lots of greens and coconut water. Then pour your smoothie into popsicle moulds and put them in the freezer for at least eight hours. Enjoy them any time of the day as a healthy, cold, and tasty treat that is providing hydration.

- Add a crystal to your drinking water container

By adding a crystal into your container, you can enhance the energies in the water. Not all crystals can be immersed in water, so make sure to check that the crystal you want to use is safe.

A Few Safe Crystals to Add to Your Drinking Water:

- Rose quartz—enhances self-love and universal love
- Clear quartz—balances and boosts immunity
- Citrine—promotes more abundance

WATER FOR CLEARING ENERGY:

We use water daily to clean our teeth, our clothes, our dishes, our food, our bodies, etc. But we can also use water to cleanse unwanted energy from our physical and emotional bodies and help ground ourselves to Mother Earth. Water can help move and wash away unwanted energies we may be experiencing from our own personal journey or energies we are clearing for the collective.

> **Personal Energies:**
> - Past traumas
> - Recent traumas
> - Ancestral traumas
> - Had a bad day
> - Overwhelmed with life circumstances
> - Daily stresses
>
> **Collective Energies:**
> - Traumas and destruction of Mother Earth
> - Global tragedies
> - Past and present wars
> - Indigenous tragedies
> - Racial and sexual tragedies
> - Suppression of the divine feminine

At this time on the planet, with the collective awakening slowly unravelling everyone's egos, we are having to face an enormous number of traumas and tragedies that have been hidden from collective knowledge. We have either turned the other way, not wanting to face the pain, or it was purposely hidden from us to carry out dark agendas. Luckily, we have water to help our bodies clear these personal and collective traumas.

Washing your hands, taking a shower or bath, going to a natural source of water and submerging your hands or whole body, or having a refreshing drink of pure and natural water can greatly benefit our bodies. There are so many different ways to interact with water! When interacting with water, in any way, we can use our intentions to ask the water for help in cleaning, clearing, and washing away things we are ready to let go. We can also bless the water and all that it will come into contact with.

SUBMERING OUR BODIES IN WATER CAN HELP:

- Relax the body
- Relax the mind (ego)
- Relax the soul
- Relax the nervous system
- Clear unwanted energies
- Recharge the body

- Relax the muscles
- Help prepare the body for sleep
- Release tension
- Lower blood pressure
- Lessen pain
- Clear energy from crystals
- Detox the pores of the skin
- Draw out toxins
- Draw out emotions
- Comfort the body, mind, and soul
- Warm the body... and the heart

WATER FOR HELP Through intention THOUGHT PRAYER

> *WATER IS SACRED*
> *WATER IS LIFE*

The Healing Powers of Water is Ancient Knowledge:

HOT SPRINGS

Human beings have used natural hot springs for ages to heal all sorts of aliments, such as skin conditions and lung problems.

HOLY WATER

Certain religions have used blessed water for centuries for protection, blessings, and baptisms.

> **Natural Water Sources:**
> - Rivers
> - Lakes
> - Ponds
> - Streams
> - Hot springs
> - Seas
> - Oceans

Natural sources of water have the ability to clear energy from our bodies and help us ground and deeply connect with nature and Mother Earth. Even just standing at the water's edge, or dipping your hands or feet with intention, can help your body release emotions and unwanted energies.

If possible, use your voice to express what it is you are ready to release. Scream, shout, and sing—loudly. Let the tears come if they want to. Say all the words your emotions want to say. Let the water wash it all away, as it has the power to cleanse darkness back into light.

SHOWERS

Easily available to most of us is a shower. With the right atmosphere and intentions, a shower can be a sacred space for relaxation, cleansing, and rejuvenation. A hot shower can lower your blood pressure, relax your tense muscles, clear your sinuses, open and clear your pores, and improve your mood.

Personally, showers are a special nightly necessity for me. It is a time just for me: A time to relax, to *love* my body with every gentle scrub of bubbles. As I take the time to wash every spot of my body, I set intentions of appreciation and love to each part of my body. I feel time slow down; I am alone and it is quiet except for the sound of rushing water. I can feel the hot water melting the tension in my muscles and washing away the physical dirt, as well as the energetic dirt I have picked up during my day. With set intentions, I will the water to cleanse away unwanted energies and bless the water as it drains away—a blessing that it may cleanse and heal all that it comes into contact with.

I use my favourite natural soap, which creates a silky lather and has an aromatic scent to add to the relaxation and enjoyment of the process. There are lots of different types of scrubbies to help create lather and exfoliate the skin.

Try to use naturally made soaps that only contain natural ingredients, even though they are expensive—your skin is worth it.

BENEFITS OF SINGING IN THE SHOWER:

- Great acoustics
- Creation of healing vibrations
- Calming—creates a good mood
- Moves energy

IT IS PRIVATE – JUST BE YOURSELF – LET GO – BE CREATIVE – HAVE FUN

It truly is the little things in life

BATHS

To me, having a bath is even more relaxing and ceremonial than showers. Baths can offer a deeper cleaning and clearing, as the body is submerged completely in the water for an extended period of time. Baths may also offer a deeper relaxation for your muscles and joints, as the body has more time to soak in the water.

Your bath could be simply hot water or it can have a bunch of other specially chosen ingredients. These added ingredients may increase your enjoyment by promoting relaxation, easing muscle or joint pain, and assisting in the clearing of unwanted energies.

> **Possible Items to Add in Water:**
> - Essential oils
> - Epsom™ salts
> - Bubble bath made with natural ingredients
> - Crystals
> - Flower petals
>
> **More Items to Add to the Atmosphere:**
> - Natural candles, such as beeswax or soy
> - Dim lighting
> - A wash cloth
> - A bath pillow
> - Soft and relaxing music
> - Large towel & housecoat

For a Relaxing and Calming Bath Add:

- 10 drops lavender essential oil
- 1 – 2 cups of Epsom™ salts
- Bubble bath made with natural ingredients
- Rose quartz and clear quartz crystals

For an Energetic Clearing Bath Add:

- 3 drops of sage essential oil
- 5 drops of frankincense essential oil
- Flower petals
- Splash of Florida water™
- Clear quartz, rose quartz, fluorite and amethyst crystals

For a Pain-Relieving Bath Add:

- 1-2 cups of Epsom™ salts
- 5 drops of rosemary essential oil
- 6 drops of peppermint essential oil

- 5 drops of patchouli essential oil
- Clear quartz and fluorite crystals

COLD WATER SUBMERSION

Though not the most popular or comfortable thing to do with water, submerging your body in very cold water is extremely beneficial for your health. Going from hot water to cold water shocks the body—in a good way. It increases circulation, which is great for many systems inside your body and also outside your body: your skin. It also boosts your immune system, increases your overall health, and promotes more resilience.

Options for Cold Water Submersion:

- Start with ten seconds—try to submerge the body from head to toe
- Gradually increase the duration
- Thirty to sixty seconds is a perfect range to aim for
- Practise this once a week or more if you want to
- Spas with hydro therapies tend to have a spot for cold water therapy
- Homemade cold-water tubs
- After a hot shower, turn the water to cold or after a bath, have a quick cold shower
- Use what nature provides: In cooler months, if possible, go to natural bodies of water such as a lake, river, or the ocean. Submerge your whole body by taking a quick dip or swim.

A short submersion in cold water strengthens the body

Chapter 4

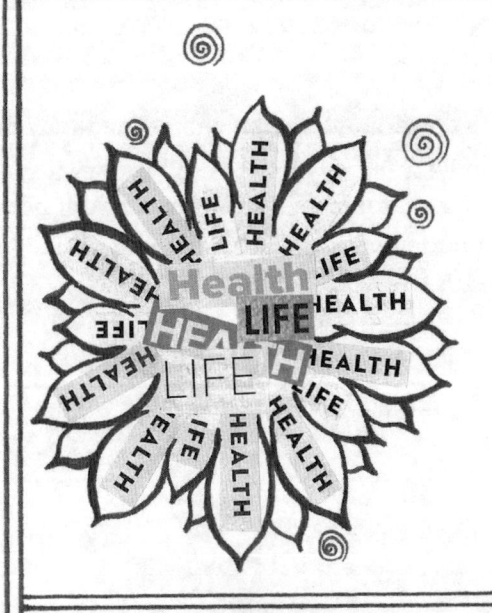

FOOD

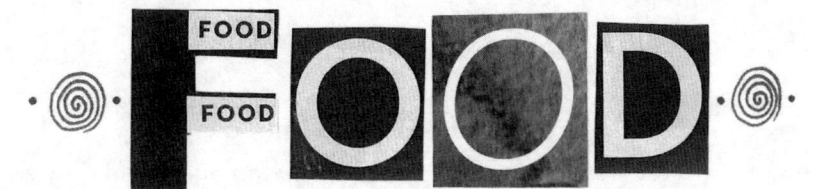

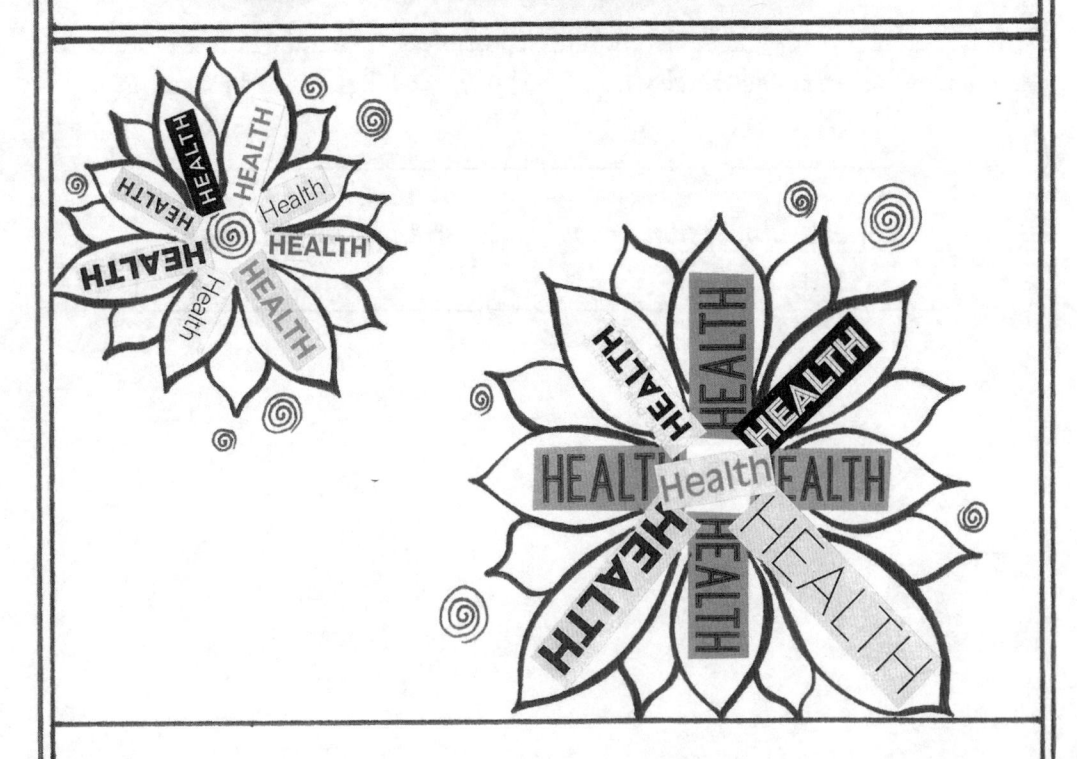

Chapter 4
FOOD

Food can be a very sensitive and triggering subject in today's world. In Western society, we have been raised with an overabundance of instant, pre-packaged foods, readily available at all hours of the day. As a society, we have fashioned food into a reward or treat. Further still, all our holidays and cultural celebrations involve food, and mostly, the unhealthy kind. We have created the *food ego*, something most of us struggle to control.

Know that you are not alone if just thinking about changing your eating habits is scary, overwhelming, or seems impossible and triggers your food ego. It can be done, however; we can change our habits. If we are brave enough to try eating healthy for an extended period of time (say three months), the benefits will be felt and seen. Experiencing all the benefits may help to re-establish a healthy, conscious relationship with food and give you motivation to continue.

But what is healthy eating? Today, so many different diets are professing to be the perfect one. Unfortunately, considering people's different body types, cultural habits, or availability of healthy and affordable food, does not seem to be well thought-out in most diets. Rather than try those diets, we should approach nutrition individually, taking into account our own body's needs, beliefs, lifestyles, and local availability. First and foremost, we have to remember that food is energy, and we need to decide what kind of energy we want to put in our bodies.

In my early thirties, it became absolutely essential to change my diet and become very conscious of what I put into my body. I had to gain new knowledge about alternative food choices, and pay attention to all labels and ingredients on anything I intended to ingest.

I had been following the standard recommended food guide for healthy eating put forth by the mainstream, but after giving birth to my daughter, no matter how healthy I ate or how much exercise I did, I could not lose the excessive weight I had gained during pregnancy. I was also suffering from various stomach problems and having increasingly unhealthy bowel movements.

After visiting a naturopath and discovering that certain foods were not agreeable with my body, I made some big changes to my diet and started listening to what my body was really craving. I cut out all gluten, dairy, and sugar from my diet for three weeks. It was life-changing, and it only took a few weeks to start feeling the full benefits. Not only did my body benefit from the change, so did my mind! I felt like a cloud cleared that had been making my brain function foggy and hampering my emotions. Most of my back pain and achy joints disappeared, and my menstrual cycles became easier, emotionally and physically. Even the extra weight from my pregnancy melted off me in a few weeks without any additional exercise.

I have continued on this path of healthy, conscious eating, though I know there is always room for improvement. Every day is a new chance to make healthier choices, but also remember to enjoy things once in a while. It is so important for our bodies and our overall health to really take a look at what we ingest, but also why. Why do we make the choices we make? Why are certain foods being over-produced and over-consumed? Why do we emotionally eat? Why do we use unhealthy foods as a reward?

It can be overwhelming and confusing to look at all the diets that are available today. A diet should not be considered a temporary thing, however. A diet needs to be seen as a healthy habit throughout a lifetime. As I stated earlier, I am not a dietitian, just a regular person, but here is my advice:

First, we need to get to know our own body type and the specific foods that will benefit and support our body's needs. Second, we need to establish a diet that fits with our lifestyle, where we live, and what is available locally. We should also mostly nourish our bodies with wholesome, fresh, and natural foods prepared with love by our own hands.

HELPFUL TIPS TO CONSIDER:

- Minimize salt and sugar intake
- Eat a variety of fresh, raw, or slightly cooked vegetables—*eat a rainbow of colours*
- Eat a moderate portion of fruits
- Drink lots of high quality water
- Avoid deep-fried foods
- Plan and prepare your own food most of the time
    - Create meal plans for the week for breakfast, lunch, dinner and snacks
    - Make a shopping list from this plan
- Cook from scratch as much as possible
- Shop locally and buy organic
- Put love and intentions in your food
    - Thank your food before, during, and after preparation
    - Thank the people that provided the food (farmers, delivery people, the cook, etc.)
    - Set an intention of clearing away all that does not belong in the food

- Set an intention of nourishing the body with all that it needs
- Prepare and cook with love, patience and nourishment as your main focus
* Keep it simple and natural—few ingredients
* Plant your own fruit trees, berry bushes, herbs, and vegetable garden

LIMIT DAIRY PRODUCTS

I never realized the number of dairy products in so many of the processed foods we eat in the western world until I started reading all the ingredient labels. It is staggering. It is alarming. It is disgusting.

When I first found out that I was allergic to dairy products made from cow's milk, I was devastated! All of my favourite foods contained dairy... pizza, lasagna, bread, ice cream. I felt overwhelmed and wondered what the hell there was left for me to eat. It definitely was a huge learning curve for me at first, but once I researched new recipes and converted old recipes, things became easier.

Through this process, I learned that goat's milk has different enzymes than cow's milk does and therefore people are seldom allergic to it. Try using goat's milk, goat butter and goat cheeses for a substitute for recipes that call for dairy products. In North America, goat products are more expensive, although this could help with moderating how much you consume.

There are also various alternatives to cow's milk that are available, such as oat, almond, cashew, macadamia, coconut, rice, and soy milk. Additionally, there are alternative options for butter, such as ghee, goat butter, or coconut oil. All of these alternatives can be used as substitutes in recipes to replace cow products.

SUGAR

One of the most harmful things we can ingest, and one of the things we easily overconsume in the world, is sugar. Today, vast amounts of high-refined sugar and corn syrup are in many pre-made products, such as in candies, baked goods, drinks, etc. If we truly look at the number of people who are suffering from diabetes and obesity, we have to admit something is not right.

Personally, when I cut out all sugar from my diet for three weeks, I could not believe how amazing I felt, all the time. I had a crazy amount of unlimited energy; my emotions were more stable; I did not have any unhealthy cravings, and I had no problem falling asleep, staying asleep, or waking up. Now, when I do indulge in a treat, I feel the effects very strongly... I feel the rush, then the crash, and then the cravings it ignites in my body and brain. As a result, I consume sugar now with a conscious awareness and limit myself to only consuming sugars of natural origins.

> **Examples of Natural Sugars:**
>
> - Fruits
> - Honey
> - Maple syrup
> - Coconut sugar
> - Xylitol
> - Molasses
> - Dates
> - Agave
> - Stevia

Since my daughter was little, sugar has negatively affected her, especially the high-refined and processed sugars. She would get extremely hyper, could not concentrate or listen and have mood swings. She would get wild eyes, dark circles under her eyes, have a gray complexion, and then crash physically and emotionally. When I became a mother, I became very aware of the insane number of opportunities children have to consume sugar. It felt like almost every month there was some holiday or celebration that involved children acquiring large quantities of high-refined sugars ... Valentine's Day, Easter, birthdays, Halloween, Christmas, and New Year's Eve.

It makes me wonder...

Why do we consume sugar as a celebration, when, in the long run, it is harming our bodies?
Why does a chemical and artificial candy have to be a reward?
Why can't an apple or carrot be a special treat or reward?

Why does food have to be treated in this manner anyways? When did something that is essential to our very survival become so unhealthy and all about enjoyment? Instead of nourishing our bodies, we turn to unhealthy food choices that slowly poison our bodies and negatively affect our lives.

The truth is, *sugar* is like a drug. When we eat sugar, the brain releases chemicals that make us, temporarily, feel good. We get a rush of energy, a buzz, and feel satisfied ... for a very limited time. Then we crash, only to crave another fix of sugar. This can create an unhealthy relationship with food and may ultimately lead to an unhealthy relationship with our bodies. We may then develop a habit of eating to improve our emotions and forget the whole purpose of eating, which is to nourish the body.

> **Emotional Eating May Lead To:**
> - Being overweight
> - An unhealthy relationship with food
> - An unhealthy relationship with the body—negative body image
> - Mood swings
> - Diabetes
> - Heart problems
> - High cholesterol
> - High blood pressure
> - Eating disorders (e.g. anorexia, bulimia, and binge eating)

SET MEAL TIMES

It is very beneficial to our bodies for us to create a routine with our meals. The body is better able to maintain a healthy blood sugar level when you eat regularly and in a healthy manner. That, in turn, can help stop overeating, unhealthy food choices, low energy, headaches, and dizziness.

To maintain a healthy lifestyle, try not to eat anything at least three hours before bedtime. The stomach needs time to rest too! If you have just eaten something and you go to bed, your poor stomach still has to stay up for a few hours to digest the food. While most of your body systems are getting their required rest and recharge, your stomach is up working late into the night. After I began to have regular, set meal times in my routine, I quickly noticed that my number twos became regular too.

SUPPLEMENTS

In our world today, even if we eat vast amounts of whole grains, fruits, and vegetables, they no longer contain the minerals and vitamins they once did. This has a lot to do with how we farm the land: we mass produce crops, use pesticides, destroy fungi systems in the soil, GMO farm, and just blatantly disrespect the soil and healthy growing practices. We have bled the earth dry, covered it with poison, and never give it proper time to naturally rejuvenate and replenish.

Much of our produce in North America now comes from around the world. We take the food from the people that live there while spreading our unhealthy and damaging system of mass food production. To travel such distances and still be good to sell, fruits and vegetables are harvested early. They are refrigerated or frozen, shipped or flown to their destination and then after they arrive, the fruits and vegetables are gassed to ripen them! With the plants not having time to reach full maturity, they hardly contain the same levels of vitamins and minerals that a properly harvest plant would contain. So, when we are eating most store-bought fruits and vegetables, our bodies are definitely missing out.

Besides eating healthy most of the time, I also take vitamins and minerals from a reputable source. Taking these supplements have really helped support my body through this Great Awakening, and all the symptoms associated with the process.

> **Examples of Supplements Available:**
> - Multi-vitamins
> - All the vitamin B's
> - Omega 3-6-9
> - Electrolytes – magnesium
> - Minerals
> - Diatomaceous Earth
> - Zeolite clay
> - Mushrooms
> - Pro-biotics and pre-biotics

Though many supplements come in pill form, they can also be found in powder form and added to drinks, such as smoothies. For many years now, my family and I have enjoyed smoothies for breakfast at least five days of the week. We invested in a professional-grade blender that can blend most things to perfection and make the ingredients easier for the body to digest.

We start our smoothies with greens (kale, spinach, Swiss chard, arugula, beet tops, or carrot tops—just use one type of green in the smoothie and change it every day), veggies (carrots and beets go nicely), fruits (bananas, apples, pears, pineapples, any type of berry, peaches, oranges, kiwis . . . to name a few of my favourites), electrolytes (coconut water), yogurt (almond, oat, or coconut yogurt), and then add any powdered supplement my body needs at the time. This is mostly decided based on my intuition, but also on any aliments my body is dealing with. Follow the guidance of your intuition, research natural supplements that will help with aliments troubling your body and use them for the recommended period of time. There can be a period of time where you take lots of supplements and then a time where you may be detoxifying and do not need to take them since your body is clearing out.

Some of my favourite powdered supplements are zeolite clay (helps clear metals out of the body), diatomaceous earth (helps clear parasites and bacteria out of the body), vitamin C and all sorts of different medicinal mushrooms. Medicinal mushrooms—such as shilajit, chaga, reishi, turkey tail, and lion's mane mushrooms—have countless benefits for the body and help with detoxifying unwanted toxins, parasites, and other things we have picked up along the way. The health benefits of medicinal mushrooms has been known and used by many cultures around the world for ages.

Having this delicious and refreshing drink for my first meal of the day gives me energy, several servings of fruits and vegetables, keeps me regular, and hydrates my whole body. Hydration is a key aspect of maintaining basic health, and many of us in the world today are highly deficient in key electrolytes, such as magnesium, and do not even know it. Magnesium deficiency, also known as hypomagnesemia, may cause muscle twitches/cramps, muscle weakness, mental numbness, an increased risk of depression, anxiety, irritability, fatigue/low energy, high blood pressure, headaches, an inability to sleep, heart palpitations, and may lead to osteoporosis.

Besides getting a pill or powdered form of magnesium, it can be found naturally in foods. Examples of foods rich in magnesium are: hazelnuts, cashews, almonds, sunflower seeds, flax seeds, chia seeds, pumpkin seeds, oats, dark chocolate, and popcorn to name a few.

Some Smoothie Recipes:

- Recipe #1 (serves 2)
    - 3 large kale leaves
    - 3 ripe bananas
    - ½ cup of coconut water
    - 1 cup of nut milk
    - 2 cups of frozen mangoes
- Recipe #2 (serves 3-4)
    - A whole carrot with tops
    - An orange
    - An apple
    - A pear
    - 1 cup of frozen pineapple chunks
    - 1 ½ cup of coconut water
    - ½ tablespoon of freshly chopped ginger
    - ½ tablespoon of freshly chopped turmeric
    - 1 cup of frozen mangoes
- Recipe #3 (serves 3-4)
    - A small beet with tops
    - 1 cup of fresh spinach
    - 1 cup of frozen strawberries

- 1 cup of frozen blueberries
- ½ cup of coconut yogurt — vanilla flavour
- ½ cup of coconut water
- 1 cup of nut milk

BODY CLEANSES AND FASTING

Between the foods we eat, the things we put on our skin, and even the very pollutants in the air around us, our bodies are continually being bombarded with metals and toxins. With this overwhelming amount of metals and toxins going into the body, our systems cannot keep up with clearing it all out. As a result, it accumulates and stores inside the body, which can lead to future health problems. But there are solutions!

One way to clear out built up metals and toxins in the body is to do a cleanse. Prepared and professionally-made cleanses are easy to find at your local health food stores. You can cleanse specific systems in your body or find whole body cleanses. Most cleanses are two weeks long, though some can last for six months to a year. During the cleanse, a set diet plan is followed to assist the body and enhance the clearing out of toxins. It is very beneficial for the body to do a cleanse once or twice a year to keep systems clear and functioning to their full potential.

BENEFITS OF A CLEANSE:

- Removes toxins and metals from the body
- Boosts your immune system
- Boosts your metabolism and can help with weight loss
- Improves energy levels
- Can help with constipation
- Can help resolve headaches, muscle aches and muscle fatigue

One of my favourite cleanses is the *Wild Rose Whole Body Cleanse*, created by Dr. Terry Willard, a clinical herbalist. This fourteen-day cleanse, like the name says, is for the whole body and specifically targets the liver, colon, kidneys, and the lymphatic system. It consists of three different pills, a tincture to be taken twice daily, and a recommended diet.

Another way of detoxifying the body is through fasting. Practised in many cultures around the world, fasting can offer a safe way of maintaining optimum health, clearing toxins from the body, and keeping all systems functioning to their best abilities. Basically, fasting is refraining from ingesting food or drinks with calories for a set period of time and consuming more than the standard eight glasses of water per day.

There are various types of fasts to try, so do some research before starting to find the right one to suit you and your lifestyle. The most popular type of fasting is called intermittent fasting and there are several options to choose from:

- Fasting for twelve hours
- Fasting for sixteen hours
- A weekly twenty-four-hour fast
- Fasting for two days
- Alternate day fasting

BENEFITS OF A FAST:

- Helps with weight loss and maintaining a healthy weight
- Can increase brain function
- Improves blood sugar control
- Helps fight inflammation
- May enhance heart health
- May increase Human Growth Hormone (HGH)
- May delay aging and extend longevity
- May aid in cancer prevention

FINAL THOUGHTS...

> *We need to change our relationship with food and nature*

Food should be selected based on what the body actually requires to function at its best, such as vitamins, minerals, antioxidants, fibre, etc. Of course, we can sometimes indulge in healthy treat options.

Personally, I try to follow a 20/80 ratio: That is, eighty percent of what I eat is healthy, naturally prepared real foods and twenty percent is healthy treats.

When our bodies have been bombarded with unhealthy foods for long periods of time and are no longer thriving, but just trying to survive on little or no nutrients, it results in unhealthy cravings and desires for "bad" foods. We can actually start craving the very things that are making our bodies sick, especially high-refined sugar and deep-fried foods.

When I did my first cleanse and ate very clean, with the only sugar I consumed from two portions of fruit per day, I started having cravings for all sorts of vegetables. Cauliflower, broccoli and carrots, to name a few, tasted amazing and satisfied my desire for food. I believe now that when I have a craving for certain vegetables or fruits, it is my body indicating what vitamins and minerals it is in need of.

> *The most important thing to remember is that food is energy*
> *Fill your body with food of the highest energy you can obtain*

CHAPTER 5

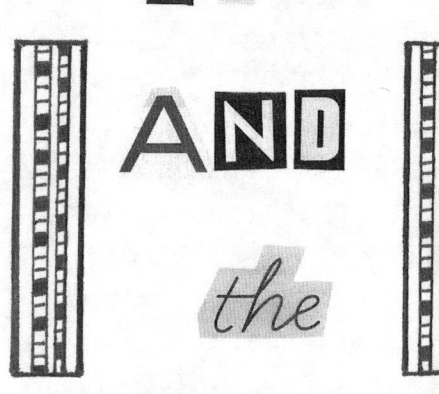

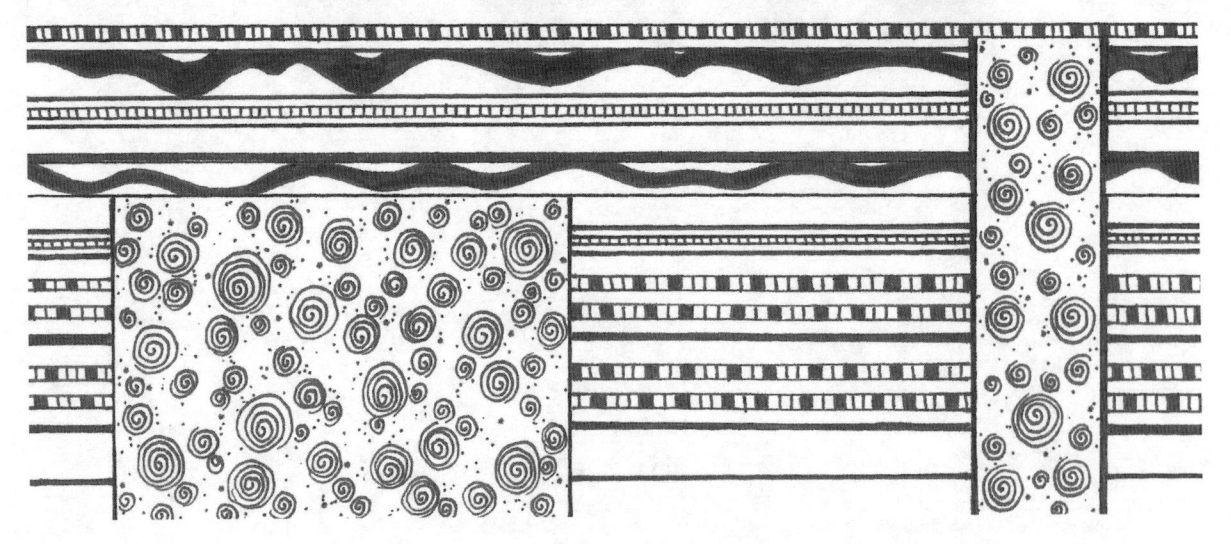

MEDITATION AND the BREATH

Chapter 5
MEDITATION AND THE BREATH

Meditation is a helpful technique to assist the mind and body during the process of the collective awakening and ascension to the 5th dimension of consciousness. Meditation promotes more peace and focus in our lives in the fast-paced and distracting world of today. Meditation can also bring up resistance, boredom, uncomfortable pains in the body, and negative thoughts.

Through modern science, we can actually see the benefits of meditation on the brain. Scientists have technologies that can take pictures and monitor the activity of brain waves during meditation. Our brain waves are electromagnetic energy that help us do so many wonderful things. There are several different states of brain waves that we can be in, though during meditation we tend to start off in Alpha wave and then as we go deeper into meditation, we enter the Theta wave.

ALPHA WAVES—aroused state of mind

- Most common state during the beginning of meditation
- Calm the nervous system
- Lower the heart rate and blood pressure
- Lower production of stress hormones
- Promote relaxation

THETA WAVES—relaxed state of mind

- Occur deeper into meditation
- Associated with the third-eye—the 6th chakra
- Help us tap into our inner, eternal wisdom
- Encourage our creativity
- Improve problem-solving skills
- Increase memory and focus
- Help keep you calm and in a balanced state of being

Various styles of meditation exist; the goal is finding the right way for *you*.

Meditation can take us deeper into a particular subject or insight, deeper into questions we are pondering, and deeper into our own subconscious and unconscious parts. Meditation may also trigger an anxious or uncomfortable and boring experience.

It is important to remember meditation is just a tool: You can set up a structured daily routine or you could meditate for a few minutes, several times throughout the day when you need a moment to centre yourself. There is no wrong way to meditate. You do not have to do it perfectly, have years of experience, or need any equipment, other than your breath. You probably already meditate and don't even realize you do it. For example, if you are walking and forget your surroundings, only to suddenly realize you have reached your destination that is meditation. You may also dance or tend a garden or create art and get lost in the actual process, with time just flying by. That, too, is meditation.

Though routines are helpful to keep us healthy and on track of our goals, it is important to remember not to let the ego take over and make it something you *have* to do. Instead, try to use meditation as a tool that you may or may not do without any consequences or judgments. Do what feels right for you at that time, and if something changes, allow your meditation practice to change as well.

SOME WAYS TO MEDITATE:

- Seated or reclined meditation
- Walking meditation
- Guided meditation
- Dance meditation
- Tree meditation
- Mantra meditation
- Mindfulness meditation

Meditation can be done with: ***closed* eyes or *open* eyes**

For *open eye* meditation, focus your eyes on:

- The flame of a candle
- A picture of a sacred symbol(s)
- A picture of a loved one or spirit guide(s)
- A sacred object
- A tree

- Mountains
- A natural body of water
- The clouds
- A flower
- A crystal
- Any stationary object in front of you

Open eye meditation encourages expanded conscious awareness and strengthens, everything we do with opened eyes

Closed eye meditation strengthens and expands our subconscious and everything we do with closed eyes

<u>*Both are beneficial*</u>

Meditate while . . . creating art, exercising, cooking, baking, cleaning, bathing
Or while . . . doing yoga, Tai Chi, Qigong

Try either:
***Focused-attention* or *open-monitoring*
MEDITATION TECHNIQUES**

POSSIBLE BENEFITS OF MEDITATION:

- Encourages relaxation of the mind and body
- Improves sleep
- Reduces anxiety
- Promotes skills to manage stress
- Decreases blood pressure
- Helps in overcoming addictions
- Increases pain tolerance
- Achieves new perspectives on life experiences
- Increases self-awareness and concentration

- Increases our attention span
- Brings more focus of the present moment
- Increases patience and tolerance
- Develops more imagination and creativity
- Reduces and assists in the processing of negative emotions
- Promotes positive emotions

POSSIBLE ITEMS TO HAVE WHILE MEDITATING:

- Pillow and blanket
- Yoga mat
- Incense/essential oil(s)
- Crystal(s)
- Candles
- Pictures of sacred symbol(s), loved one(s) or spirit guide(s)
- A sacred object
- Calming music
- A drum
- Or have nothing but you and your breath

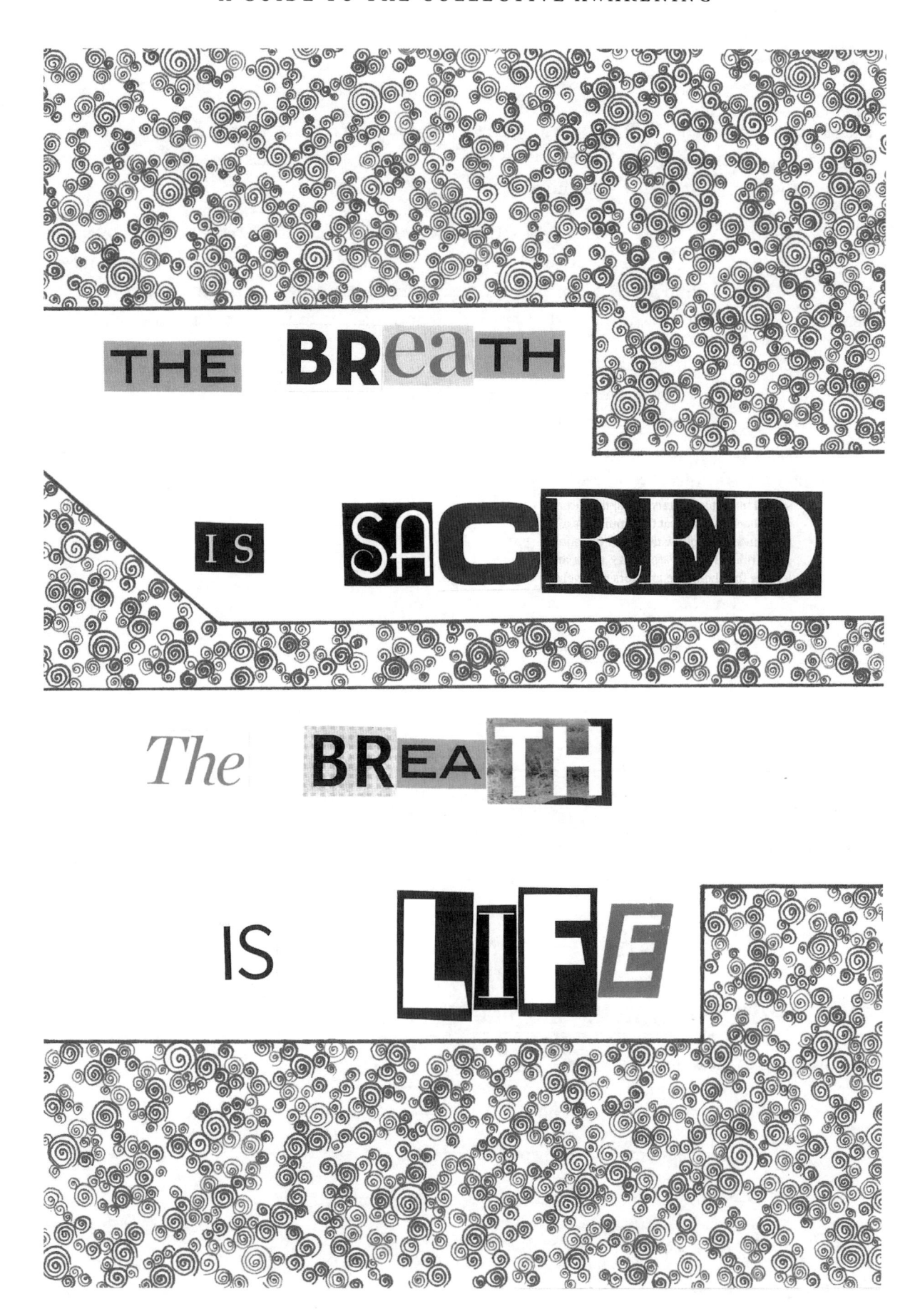

THE BREATH

IS SACRED

The BREATH

IS LIFE

THE BREATH

The breath is essential to life. It is something that just naturally occurs on its own. In and out, in and out it goes, effortlessly maintaining its rhythm. The breath can tell us about someone—their level of fitness or their mood. It is truly something we cannot live without.

Breathing during meditation can simply be automatic. You can allow the brain to control the rate of your breathing, and not give it any focus or attention. Alternatively, your meditation could have the breath as the main focus of the practice and experience. Regardless, it is beneficial to take at least three big, deep breaths at the start of any meditation practice to help you relax and achieve a focused state.

There are various different breathing techniques that are associated with traditional yoga practices in India. They are called pranayama and have been present in India since around 5000 BC. In Sanskrit, prana means "breath" or "life force" and ayama means "to control." In a traditional Indian yoga practice, pranayama are considered a fundamental aspect of yoga, just as important as the yoga poses, called asana. In the modern world, pranayama (breath work) is an integral part of all forms of different yoga practices, such as kundalini, hatha, and Ashtanga.

BREATHING TECHNIQUES

POPULAR PRANAYAMA BREATHING TECHNIQUES:

- Dirga—three-part breath
- Nadi sodhana—alternate nostril breathing
- Ujjayi—ocean breath
- Kapalabhati—breath of fire

OTHER TYPES OF BREATHING TECHNIQUES:

- Abdominal breathing technique
    - Inhale deeply and focus on your belly fill and rise
    - Exhale deeply and focus on your belly deflate and fall
    - Try to do a cycle of fifteen to thirty deep inhales and exhales
    - Return to normal breathing, then repeat the cycle
- Timed breath focus

- Inhale for four seconds, through the nose
- Hold the breath in for seven seconds
- Exhale for eight seconds, through the mouth
- Hold the breath out for four seconds
- Repeat this cycle at least four times

- The Wim Hof Method

The WHM is a combination of exposure to cold water, breathing exercises, and meditation. The exposure to cold water is known to strengthen the cardiovascular system and the immune system. Wim Hof suggests, after a hot shower, switch to cold water for fifteen seconds and over the course of four weeks increase to two minutes.

The breathing exercises are known to increase energy levels and change the body's chemistry. For a detailed and personal explanation from Wim Hof, himself, visit his website www.wimhofmethod.com.

POSSIBLE BENEFITS OF PRACTISING BREATHING TECHNIQUES:

- Less stress
- Less anxiety
- Better sleep
- Increased lung function
- Improved cardiovascular health
- Enhanced concentration
- Management of blood pressure
- Release of pent-up emotions and energy

> *Never stifle a yawn ... It is a natural way of releasing energy from the body*

For me, meditating and breath work have always been about quieting my mind and creating a space away from the constant chatter of the world, my ego, or thoughts buzzing around my mind. It is about taking a moment in time where I put everything else to the side and just breathe. It is almost like reaching a still point of my being, where it is peaceful and calm, like a space of nothingness. There is nothing to do, nothing to know, and nothing to figure out. Sometimes, simply taking a moment to breathe deeply—go beyond the busyness and stresses of daily life—can rejuvenate, promote a calm state, and open up fresh new perspectives.

Just remember to *not* let it become another thing the ego latches onto, tries to control, and then uses against you if you don't do it. If you feel called to set up a routine and find it significantly benefitting you, great! Meditation or practising a breathing technique works best only as long and as often as it feels right and helpful in your life. Be open to constantly changing and adapting your practice as you flow through your journey of life. If one day you don't feel called to meditate or do focused breathing work in the same way, it is okay to let it go and try something completely new. You can always come back to previous techniques you've done when and if you feel called to.

> There is **no** obligation to have a set purpose to achieve
> Or goals to accomplish
> Through meditation and breathing techniques
> Just create some space and time for *you*
> This is **your** time
> **Your** experience
> Whatever *you* need in the moment...
> To stop a busy mind
> Calm down
> Centre yourself
> Strengthen your focus and attention span
> Relax your nervous system
> Or simply
> Be aware of the present moment

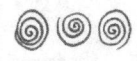

FINAL THOUGHTS...

A few years ago, for three months, I meditated with a tree every day for twenty minutes. I would pick a tree, lay a small blanket down to sit on, and set a timer. The timer helped me let go of having to keep track of the time. I had other responsibilities, so I couldn't just meditate for hours (though I wanted to). If the weather was too wet for my liking, I would sit at a window and gaze at a tree. The experience was beautiful and rejuvenating. I felt an extreme sense of calm and relaxation come over me within just a few minutes and a deep connection to the refreshing nature surrounding me. Every day, I looked forward to it and was excited to find the tree I would spend this special silent time with. After doing this tree meditation every day for several months, without fail, it suddenly started to feel like a chore. My ego had taken over, and I felt pressured to do it. If I was unable to do it, I felt like I had failed and judged myself for it. So, I just let the whole thing go. I stopped meditating daily with a tree and felt the pressure and judgments lift. I knew I would meditate and breathe with trees again, but only when the desire arose in me or I felt a need to be with the trees (which is often) —not because I had to.

As I have progressed in my meditation and breathing practices, it has become more of an automatic state I drop in and out of during my days. When I feel my body or mind tensing up or becoming overwhelmed, I can pick a technique that fits the moment and give myself a few minutes of aligning with a state of peacefulness and calm. A lot of times, this happens in the bathroom where I get rare moments of alone time.

In our modern society, everything is GO, GO, GO. There is so much going on all the time, from all angles and areas in our lives. We are all over-stimulated, and this is extremely hard on our immune systems and our nervous systems. Meditation and breathing techniques can help slow down our mind and body, even for just a few minutes at a time. Giving yourself these few minutes to breathe and clear your thoughts of anything can help you regain a state of calm and relaxation. It does not have to be elaborate, strenuous or time consuming; instead, make it fit you and *your* lifestyle.

CHAPTER 6

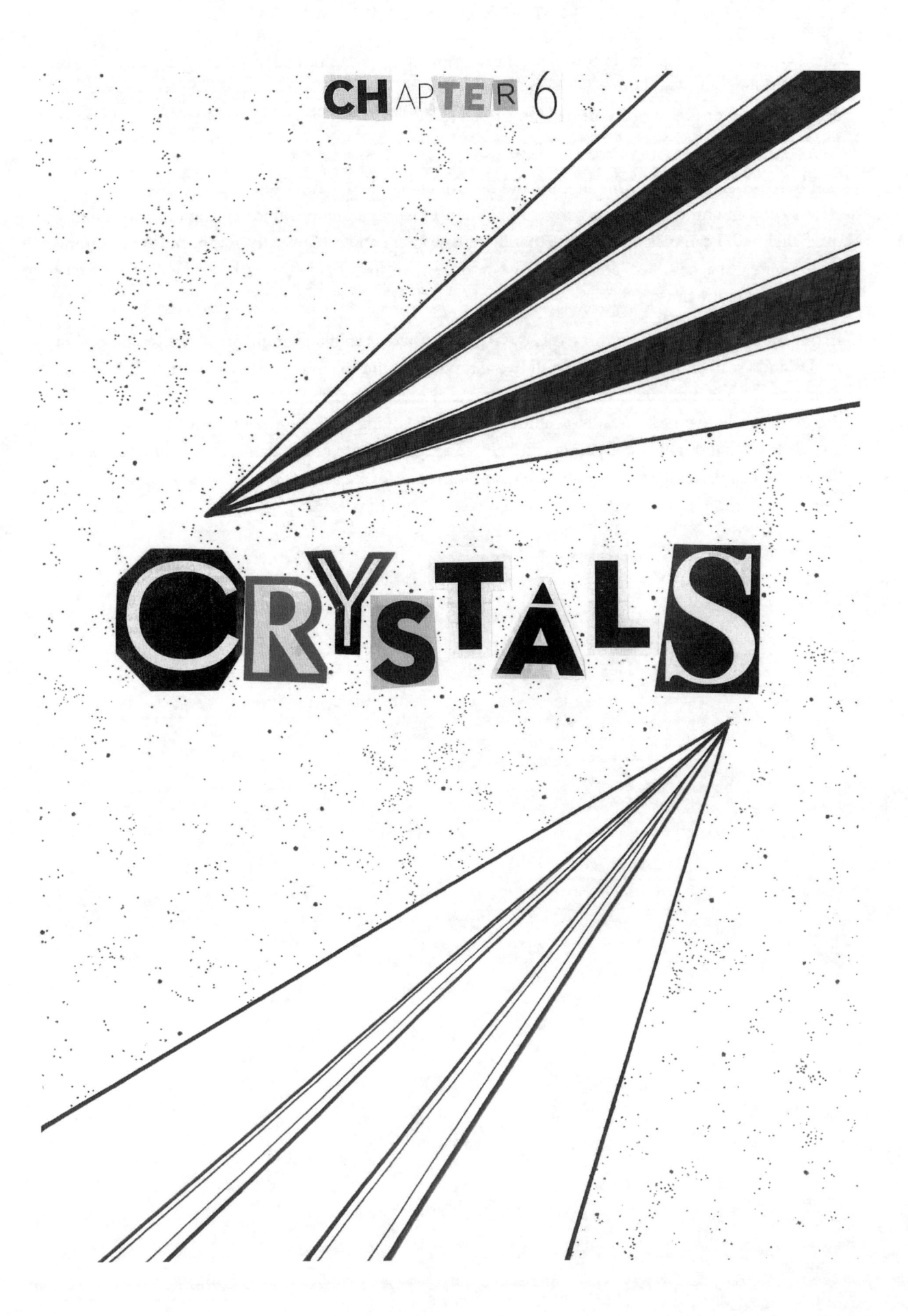

CRYSTALS

Chapter 6
CRYSTALS

> *Crystals are alive*
> *Born and thriving*
> *Deep within Mother Earth*
> *Slowly growing*
> *For millions of years*

Crystals offer a unique assistance at this time of the collective awakening and ascension process underway on Earth. Among other things, crystals reconnect the modern human being to themselves, to Mother Earth, and the divine Universe beyond. Crystals promote the flow of positive and harmonious energies to all the sentient beings around their proximity. They can absorb and store information, respond to the inputs of all sorts of energies nearby them, and they emit a specific kind of vibratory frequency. Because of this, crystals are used in various types of modern technologies, such as cell phones, computers, TVs, and satellites.

Crystals have existed under the Earth's surface for millions of years. They have been gathered and used by human beings for a very, very long time for various purposes. Crystals have been used in ancient burial rites, healing rituals, divination practices, for spiritual advancement, and as a decoration and symbol of power all over the world, in many different cultures. It is no wonder why crystals are so popular and still being widely used by so many today.

Each crystal has its own unique colour, quality, ability, and attribute. They can help rid the mind and body of negative energies and help heal and support physical, mental, and emotional ailments. Some crystals can protect and shield against negative energies and even promote brain function. Also, crystals have the ability to help increase concentration and the intake of knowledge.

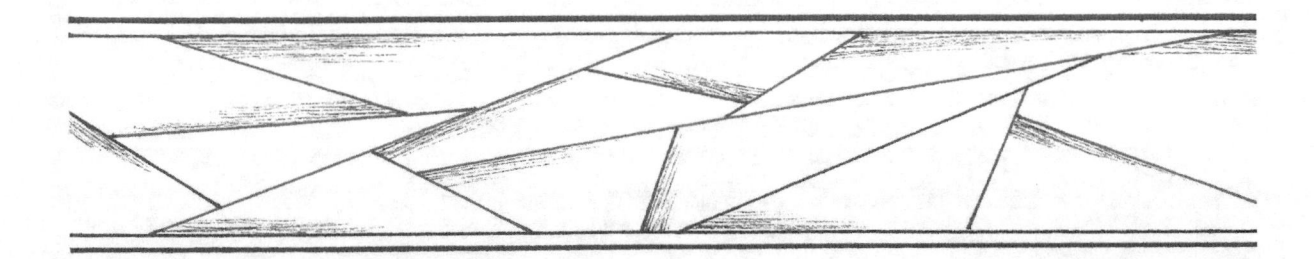

REMOVED from Place OF ORIGIN

CRystals ARE Still ALIVE

if Left

UNTOUCHED & unMOVED

Some CryStals

CONTINUE TO GROW

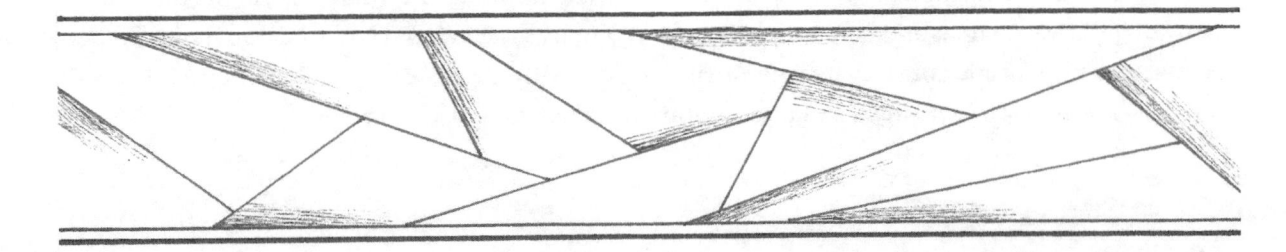

For as long as I can remember, I have been drawn to rocks, fossils, and most of all, crystals. I realized later, after learning more about the energy fields around all living things, that I was being drawn toward and attracted by the energies of these pieces of Mother Earth.

With certain crystals, I would sense a warm feeling of flowing energy in parts of my body and have a strong desire to hold and acquire them. I quickly established a small collection of crystals, mostly smaller pieces that I could easily move around or carry with me. I soon became attuned to each of their unique energies on a deeper conscious level and developed a sense, a line of communication with them. It was not a voice speaking; there was no sound. The interaction is more like thoughts that pop into my head, such as "pick me up" or "hold me." Mostly, it is through my feelings that I communicate and exchange information with crystals.

As time went on and my collection has grown, I have become more and more attuned with the crystals that live with me. Many times, I will be getting ready to leave home and suddenly I will think of a certain crystal and know that it wants to be close to me. I have a small pouch of crystals in my purse and have worn many different crystals on my body when the desire presented itself… or should I say, when the crystal expressed the desire and I listened.

I love the versatility of crystals and the ability to bring them with you, anywhere. It is nice to have larger pieces in your home or office, but I really appreciate the smaller pieces that can be made into jewelry, put in my vehicle, placed under my pillow or bed, dropped in my drinking water, or carried in a pocket. This versatility makes it easy to have direct contact with them and reap the benefits of their energies, no matter where I am.

CRYSTALS IN DRINKING WATER?!

Yes, it is true!

Immersed crystals in water create an effortless and excellent way to work with and integrate their energies. The energies from the crystals can be absorbed into the water and then consumed, deepening the connections gained and the energies received.

Not all crystals are safe to put in drinking water! Be sure to research any crystal you intend to use. Some crystals dissolve in water.

Common Crystals to Put into Drinking Water:

- Rose quartz
- Clear quartz
- Smoky quartz
- Aventurine
- Jasper
- Black Obsidian
- Amethyst
- Tiger's Eye

Crystals have supported me through various aspects and phases of my life. They have helped me face and clear intense emotions like fear, loneliness, anxiety, and sadness. Being a very open-hearted empath, who is sensitive to all energies, it can be very intense to be around other people at times. Crystals have assisted me immensely in blocking, clearing, and integrating many of the energies I have faced along my journey.

For most of my life, as an energetically sensitive being, I have been aware of negative energies coming off of people, electronic devices, and Mother Earth itself. With people, I can feel their internal energies and the energies they send out, whether they are loving or filled with pain and anger. Electronic devices also emit energies and sounds that I have personally found unsettling, disruptive, and harmful. The energies of intense suffering and anguish emitting from Mother Earth, however, are by far the strongest and most overwhelming to witness. Luckily, I discovered crystals (or they found me), and they offer me support during these interactions with energies surrounding me.

For a long period of time, I have loved black crystals, such as obsidian, Apache tear, jet or black tourmaline. I sensed their ability to ground me and provide support when I was around negative energies. They would block the negative energies from entering my energy field and continually transmute it all back into the light. I have a very powerful star energy force within me and feel myself often "up in the clouds." Black crystals help bring my energy back into my body and ground it deep into Mother Earth.

I have also always been extremely attracted to rose quartz and its powerful love energy. When feeling sad, lonely, anxious, or overwhelmed, I hold a rose quartz crystal in my hands and a supportive, loving, calm feeling floods my heart and encircles my body. Rose quartz has helped me grow love in all aspects of my life. By just spending time around its energies, the feelings of self-love, love for others, and unconditional love that already exist inside me, have been amplified.

HOW TO PICK CRYSTALS

If you feel the desire to acquire a crystal, but aren't sure how to pick the "right" one, just know that you cannot get it wrong. You will probably be drawn to various crystals, either by the way they look, their colour, their texture, or the way they make you feel. Listen and pay close attention to your responses; this is your intuition communicating to you, or possibly even the crystals trying to connect with you.

Today, it is easy to acquire all sorts of crystals from anywhere in the world. You can shop online or at local shops. Personally, I prefer to see crystals in-person. This enables me to hold and examine them closely. I love visiting crystal shops, local markets, or spirit fairs to find my crystals. At that time, I can speak directly with the seller that purchased the crystals. This is important because first, you want to be sure the crystals are not fake and secondly, that they come from a reputable dealer. With the popularity of crystals on the rise, some people are unfortunately more focused on making money than on the quality of the crystals, where they come from, or how they were retrieved from the earth.

If you are able to go to a local shop, before entering, try to have an intention or idea of what you are seeking from the crystals you intend to acquire. Are you seeking help with grounding or protection, increasing abundance in all aspects of life or amplifying feelings of love? Do you need help with clearing energies within or around you to protect you while travelling, or are you trying to connect to your spirit guides on a deeper level?

First, I recommend walking around the shop and having a quick look at what is available. Then, using all of your senses, focus on opening up to any subtle thoughts, urges, or feelings you may have. Is there a crystal that is extremely visually pleasing to you? Is there one that has a special or significant shape, colour, or size? If something does appeal to you, I suggest picking it up and holding it in your hands. Take a few deep breaths, and using all of your senses, look at it and touch it. Then close your eyes and see if you have any visuals in your "minds-eye" or if any thoughts or ideas come into your present awareness.

For online shopping, you could modify these previous suggestions, though you will not be able to touch the crystals. Instead, use your intuition, your eyes, and your feelings to help guide you in your choices. That "gut" feeling, or strong desire could be your body deeply resonating and connecting with a certain crystal. Listen to it, and do not second guess these subtle messages.

Also, when you first acquire the crystals, it is very important to clean and charge them! After possibly travelling the world to reach their destination, then sitting in a shop and being handled by various people, the crystals are full of unwanted energies. Later in this chapter you will find suggestions on cleaning and charging crystals.

POSSIBLE WAYS TO CONNECT WITH CRYSTALS:

- May feel warm in your hands
- Strongly appeals to you visually
- Tingling sensation in parts of the body or whole body
- A buzzing in any of your chakra areas
- A surge of emotions—love, support, comforting
- Feelings of friendship or familiarity
- Specific thoughts about the crystal popping into your consciousness

> *Trust your intuition . . .*
> *Listen for the soft messages*
> *The whispers in the calm*

Ultimately, there exists many different reasons to acquire crystals, and all crystals, in some way or another, may assist in various aspects of your life. The key is not to get overwhelmed by the number of available choices, or forget the main reason you are looking for one in the first place. Hold your focus on your intentions and don't get distracted by all the beauty you will see. All crystals have a purpose and are incredibly beautiful to the human eye, so be prepared to want them all.

When I am around a lot of crystals, it can be very intense and overwhelming if I do not stay grounded and focused on my initial intent. At the same time, I want to be open to new possibilities that I may not have even considered or knew existed.

SOME OF MY FAVOURITE CRYSTALS:

MOLDAVITE

Colour: light to dark olive green

Associated with the 5th, 6th and 7th chakras

Attributes:

- Created when a meteorite crashed into the Earth 14.8 million years ago
- Nicknamed "The Stone of Transformation"
- Enhances the third eye, inner vision
- Attunement and connection to higher self and higher dimensions
- Strengthens psychic abilities and intuition

BLACK OBSIDIAN

Colour: black

Associated with the 1st chakra

Attributes:

- Helps with grounding deep into Mother Earth
- Potent cleanser
- Provides powerful psychic protection
- Contains powerful healing energies

ROSE QUARTZ

Colour: light pink

Associated with the 4th chakra

Attributes:

- Promotes positive energies
- Enhances all types of love (self, for others and unconditional)
- Raises self-esteem and helps build confidence
- Assists in balancing emotions
- Helps release stress, tension, and anger

CLEAR QUARTZ

Colour: clear, glass-like

Associated with the 7th chakra

Attributes:

- Extremely powerful at clearing energies
- Master healer
- Amplifies energies, thoughts, and vibrations of other crystals
- Helps with connecting to your higher self, intuition, and spirit guides

AMETHYST

Colour: purple

Associated with the 6th and 7th chakra

Attributes:

- Clears negative energies from within and around you
- Relieves stress and anxiety
- Helps with connecting to higher plains of existence
- Strengthens your intuition

CITRINE

Colour: ranges from light brown to smoky clear to yellow/amber

Associated with the 3rd chakra

Attributes:

- Enhances and inspires creativity

- Promotes wealth and abundance
- Stimulates personal power and self-confidence
- Helps establish healthy boundaries in all areas of life

FLUORITE

Colour: can be blue, yellow, pink, red, orange, purple, green, brown, black, or clear

Associated with the 3rd chakra

Attributes:

- Absorbs and clears negative energy
- Relieves stress from the mind and body
- Promotes learning and the ability to take in information
- Strengthens concentration
- Inspires self-confidence and intuition
- Balances energies within the body and mind

TURQUOISE

Colour: blue, blue-green, green

Associated with the 5th chakra

Attributes:

- Creates a bridge between higher realms and Mother Earth
- Opens and connects the mind to the infinite possibilities of the divine Universe
- Master healer
- Connects you with the healing energies of water
- Promotes a state of calm and tranquility

CLEANING CRYSTALS

It is very important to clean crystals of energies they have accumulated so as to keep them vibrating high in their natural positive energies. Crystals absorb and retain the information of all the energies around them, so cleaning them clears away unwanted or stagnant energies.

There are many ways to safely, quickly, and easily clean your crystals with natural and readily available materials, such as natural water sources and rice. Remember, some crystals **do not** like to be in contact with water! Water can destroy and dissolve certain crystals, so be sure to research any crystals you intend to put in water. Some crystals to keep in mind that do not like water are: selenite, amber, turquoise, moonstone, calcite, azurite, and angelite.

EIGHT WAYS TO CLEAN CRYSTALS:

1 – NATURAL BODIES OF WATER

Take your crystals to a small stream, a river, the ocean, the sea, or set them out in the rain.

Sometimes I hold the crystals in my hands and immerse them in flowing water. I may also place them on the sand where the waves gently reach the shore or on the banks of a gentle flowing river. I have even gathered some sea water in a shell, placed my crystals inside and set it in the sand for a while.

Do what makes you feel comfortable. Take extra care of crystals around flowing water, as they can easily get lost and become a gift for the water.

You can even ask crystals how they would prefer you to facilitate a thorough cleaning. Simply ask, then be open to any thoughts, feelings or impulses you might have. Remember, you might not hear or have new thoughts. It might be very subtle and very quiet; follow your intuition.

If you are unable to access natural bodies of water, you could try cleansing your crystals by placing them in a bowl with a mixture of water and one teaspoon of high-quality sea salt. Let the crystals soak for at least a few minutes, then take them out and rinse well. Either gently dry with a cloth or leave them to air dry.

2 – BURIED IN DIRT

Dirt, or earth, is extremely efficient at absorbing and clearing unwanted energies from crystals. Simply find a safe spot to bury your crystals in the earth for at least a few hours where they will not be disturbed. Your backyard, or somewhere close to your home, is convenient and safe, but burying them in a local forest, garden, or park is also an option. Make sure to leave some sort of marker on the surface so you can retrieve them easily.

3 – SACRED SMOKE

For millennia, various cultures all over the world have used sacred smoke to purify and clear away unwanted energies from people, places, and objects. In North America, many Indigenous people burn sacred dried plants, such as cedar, sage, sweet grass, and tobacco. This practice is known as smudging. In South America, they burn the wood from the sacred Palo Santo tree and also use the smoke from Mapacho, a sacred black tobacco for protection, healing, and clearing of negative energies. In many Eastern cultures, they use the smoke from handmade incense sticks or cones to purify and cleanse unwanted energies from homes and scared places.

It is important to remember where these practices originally come from and use them with respect and acknowledgement of the cultures they came from. Many of the beautiful Indigenous, or First Peoples, of the globe have faced atrocities beyond comprehension. The harmonious connection to nature and deep spirituality that was already a way of life for Indigenous cultures across the planet, is now what many are trying to get back to. Amazingly enough, much of the ancient wisdom from these cultures is being shared openly, in the hopes of changing the current destructive path we are on.

It is essential to set up a safe, controlled, and properly ventilated area when practising sacred smoke clearings. Most dried plants intended for burning will be gathered and tied in a tight bundle. Other larger pieces, such as tree bark or sticks of wood, are ready to use. Along with your chosen sacred plant, have a fire-resistant vessel to gather the ashes and possible embers that may fall off during the process, such as a shell, ceramic pot or a glass or metal container.

To create the sacred smoke, start by lighting one end of the sacred plant bundle or stick with a small flame and let it burn for a few seconds. Then, blow out the flame and continue to blow on the hot embers to help them grow. Make sure to have your fire-resistant vessel on hand to catch any failing embers and ashes. With your hands, or a special feather, waft the sacred smoke around your crystals and immerse them in the smoke for a few minutes. Use your intentions, thoughts, or prayers to ask the sacred smoke to purify and clear away all unwanted and negative energies from the crystals.

Once you have finished, be sure to completely extinguish any embers still burning or smoking, before putting them away for future use. Take the ashes gathered in your chosen vessel and discard them outside, in the dirt.

4 – RICE

Rice is incredible at absorbing and drawing out unwanted energies from crystals and returning them to their natural core frequency. Rice resonates with the energy of the sun and the earth, which is useful for re-balancing the natural energies in crystals. Symbolically, rice represents numerous aspects of a full and balanced life.

Find a container for the rice and the crystals you intend to clean, preferably a glass or wooden container. Make sure the container is deep enough to fully immerse the crystals in the rice. Fill the container with uncooked dry brown rice, then bury your crystals completely in the rice. Set the container somewhere it will be undisturbed for at least twelve hours, possibly even overnight. A window sill is an ideal spot, since it is also being exposed to the sun and moon energies and is out of the way.

After the twelve- to twenty-four-hour immersion, remove all the crystals from the rice. I recommend you **throw the rice away**. There are some people who keep the rice and reuse it for various things, like making rice water, eating or bathing. I, personally, would discard of the rice and the unwanted energies it has absorbed. Follow your intuition on how you want to deal with the used rice; there is no wrong way.

5 – THE MOON AND THE SUN

Moonlight and sunlight contain powerful waves of energies capable of cleansing and charging all that comes into contact with their rays. Moonlight is considered safer to cleanse crystals with because it is much more delicate, and crystals can be left in the rays of the moonlight for long periods of time with no damaging effects. Also, the powerful rays of a full moon offer a reminder of natural cycles, assistance with grounding, and balance energies, all of which is helpful when working with crystals.

For moonlight cleansing, simply gather the crystals and place them directly in the rays of the moonlight. This could be on a window sill or outside on your patio, in your garden, or your backyard where they can absorb the full rays for the whole duration of nightfall. It is most beneficial to do this during a full moon, when the moonlight is at its brightest, though any time in the lunar cycle will also work. The rays of the moon continuously touch and support Mother Earth and those upon her.

Sunlight, on the other hand, has intense rays that can actually damage or cause discolouration to some crystals. Therefore, it is very important to only expose your crystals to sunlight for very short periods of time. On a bright sunny day, gather the crystals and place them directly in the rays of the sunlight for **only a few minutes**. Hold them out in your hands, put them in a window sill, or place them in your garden or backyard.

6 – INTENTIONS OR PRAYERS

Our thoughts and intentions are so powerful. They have a huge impact on the life that we create for ourselves and those around us. They have the ability to develop, first into ideas and then into beliefs we hold, and ultimately, become the reality we perceive. We can also use our thoughts and intentions to influence people, plants, animals, and other sentient life around us.

Also powerful is the influence of prayer. A prayer is a compilation of words, feelings, emotions, desires, life-force energy, and love. Prayer is very similar if not the same as intentions. Both are focused thought and energy, usually with the purpose of reaching a goal, getting answers, or gaining support.

> *Through both*
> *Intentions and prayers*
> *We*
> *Harness and direct-out*
> *Our*
> *Divine life-force energy*
> *Into that which*
> *We*
> *Intend or pray for*

JENNA WALKER

INTENTIONS & PRAYERS TRAVEL

FAR, FAR, FAR DISTANCES

ACROSS OCEANS

through WALLS

DEEP INTO people's HEARTS & Minds

THIS IS One OF Our DIVINE POWERS

Crystals can be cleansed of unwanted energies with the power of your intentions and prayers. I would suggest that a close connection should already be established with the crystal to strengthen the power of your intentions or prayers.

With this deep connection to the crystal, and your divine healing energies, you can set intentions and prayers for clearing from a space of love. Hold the crystal in your hands (or if too large, place your hands on its surface), and with a few deep breaths, bring yourself into a meditative state. Then, either out loud or in your head, speak words from your heart, possibly with guidance from the crystal itself. Speak the words you feel are appropriate for the clearing or feel guided to say.

You could use words such as:

Clear, cleanse, change, purge, transmute, return, transform, blessings

Or, say things like:

"It is my intention, with my loving energy, to clear all unwanted energies from this crystal, return them to the light of the divine Universe (or Source or archangel or your higher self or other spirit guides). And so it is."

"With the powers of the divine Universe, and my intentions of clearing, may all unwanted energies within and around this crystal be returned to the light. And so it is."

7 – SELENITE CRYSTAL

The crystal selenite is known for its strong cleansing and purification properties. Selenite can be used to clear unwanted energies from other crystals simply by being in close proximity or having quick contact.

Selenite can come in wand shapes, large flat slabs, and smaller irregular shapes. The wand shape is useful for easy holding and touching other crystals with the other end. Large flat slabs work well for setting other stones upon it for an extended period of time.

Besides selenite, large quartz clusters and amethyst geodes are also very useful in cleansing other smaller crystals. These large crystals naturally have very immense and powerful vibrations.

8 – ORGONE DEVICES

Orgone devices are man-made energy cleansers that are composed with an organic material surrounding and compressing metals. Generally, they are made with resin and copper, though many contain crystals as well. When the metal is compressed, a powerful vortex is created with the ability to clear stagnant and unwanted energies.

It all started with Wilhelm Reich and his scientific discoveries from the early nineteenth century. Reich discovered and provided scientific proof that every living thing has a blue energy field around it. He called it *orgone* energy. Further into Reich's research, he discovered different types of orgone energy: POR (positive orgone energy) such as the vibration of love, and DOR (deadly orgone energy) such as radiation, EMFs, and the vibration of anger.

Through various experiments, Reich discovered that compressed metal creates a vortex capable of changing the DOR energy back into POR energy. He designed and manufactured various devices that he used to treat all sorts of aliments in people, with extraordinary results. One of these devices, called an Orgone Accumulator, was a large rectangular structure that a person could sit inside on a chair. It was constructed with layers of wood and metal compressed tightly together.

Sadly, due to the simplicity, affordability, and exceptional healing abilities of Reich's Orgone Accumulators, his science was attacked, destroyed, and deemed illegal. Luckily, Reich's science and knowledge survived these brutal and unlawful attacks. It was around 1960 when the hidden knowledge resurfaced. People from all over the world started to hand-make orgone devices based on Reich's science and designs. Today, instead of wood, resin is the most commonly used material in creating orgone devices. Resin is extremely versatile and easy to work with. As a result, various shapes and sizes can be made simply. Also, resin is transparent, so all the materials inside are visible. With modern orgone devices, crystals and copper coils are generally added, along with the metals to amplify their abilities.

Orgone devices have the ability to relieve and possibly eliminate things like depression, anxiety, and insomnia in people and animals. They can be used to purify the energy of water and help plants grow bigger and healthier. Today, most people who acquire orgone devices use them to help clear and protect their bodies from radiation, EMFs, and other stagnant, unwanted energies.

So, for *crystals* . . .

Orgone devices are extremely helpful with clearing and harmonizing the natural energies of crystals. Simply place the orgone device near or touching the crystal for at least a few minutes. Follow your own intuition or guidance from the crystal as to how long of a duration is needed with the transmuting vortex of the orgone device.

CHARGING AND PROGRAMMING CRYSTALS

After purifying and clearing your crystals of any unwanted energies, it is very important to charge them with new, clean, powerful, and high-vibrational life-force energies. This will assist the crystals in bringing forth their own specific qualities and inherent potent energies. The process of cleaning the crystals will make their energies stronger, more powerful, and harmonious.

With a freshly clean crystal, it is also important to program them with your own personal intentions. Crystals have powerful abilities to store and process energies around them, but they need direction. Through your words, thoughts, and intentions, you can let them know where to focus their energy for deeper healing and interaction.

FOUR WAYS TO CHARGE CRYSTALS:

1 – THE MOON

As discussed before, the rays of the moonlight contain powerful energies that benefit and affect all life on Mother Earth. During the full moon, the rays are at their strongest vibration, which makes it a perfect time to harness that energy into your crystals.

Gather your crystals the day of the full moon and decide where to set them up that will allow the most direct rays of the moonlight.

One option is to take your crystals directly outside and place them somewhere safe to leave them overnight, if possible. A few hours is enough time if you do not want to leave them out overnight. Find a spot on a table, the grass, the dirt, a piece of wood, or on a patio or deck. Use your intentions to ask that the moon's rays charge your crystals with its powerful and healing energies. Follow your intuition; ask for the qualities, attributes, and energies that you desire or need help with. Use whatever words come to you—you cannot get this wrong. Be open, be silly. Let go of your doubts or worries. Be in the moment. Believe. Breathe. Connect. Stare at the moon for a few minutes and focus on the light vibrating off of it. Talk with the moon. Feel it. Be open to it. Embrace its radiant light. Listen to its messages.

When you feel done and have filled your crystals with all that you had intended, it is time to thank the moon and its energies. Again, using your intuition, say the words of gratitude you feel within your heart. It does not have to be complicated; it can be as simple as "thank you." Just be authentic with your words and speak from the heart. When finished expressing your gratitude, either leave the crystals in their place overnight or gather them up and return them inside.

The second option is to place your crystals on a window ledge that has access to direct moonlight for at least a few hours. In the early evening, find the best window with the most amount of moonlight available and place your crystals on the ledge. Later, when the moonlight is shining on the crystals, follow the steps from the first option: set intentions, follow your intuition, be open, breathe, and connect. Make sure to thank the moon and its powerful energies. Then, you can either gather up your crystals and put them away or leave them on the ledge overnight.

2 – THE SUNLIGHT

As discussed before, the sunlight is a very powerful source of divine life-giving energy that can be used to charge crystals. Remember that the sunlight is very strong and can damage or cause discolouration in some crystals. However, because the sunlight is so potent and powerful, only a short exposure is needed to reap the benefits.

On a bright, sunny day, gather the crystals you want to charge and bring them outside. You can simply hold them out in your hands, or place them on the grass, in the dirt, on a tree or table—**only for a few minutes**. Follow your intuition, ask for the qualities, attributes, and energies that you desire or need help with. Call upon the rays of the sun to charge the crystals with its powerful energies. Again, be open, breathe, and connect. Then, thank the sun and its energies with authentic words spoken from your heart and return the crystals to their current home.

3 – THE EARTH AND MOUNTAINS

The planet itself has incredible energies—energies that will ground, rejuvenate, and centre all living beings with the right heart-space and intentions. Crystals are created in and of the earth, so it only seems natural that they are deeply connected with the planet and its divine energies.

Mountains contain incredible energies as well. The high peaks on mountains reach up into the skies and radiate powerful energies. All beings that visit these places, high in the mountains, will bask and absorb the high vibrations of energy. Crystals love to reconnect with the natural energies of the earth, making it a perfect place for them to charge and regain their base vibrations.

Gather up the crystals you would like to charge and take them out into nature, maybe to a forest, the beach, a park, a meadow, by a river or lake, or even just in your own backyard. Make sure the crystals directly touch the earth. Set them in the sand, the grass, the dirt, on a rock, in a shell, or on a tree. Using your intuition as guidance, ask Mother Earth to charge your crystals with its divine life-giving, grounding, and rejuvenating energies. Leave the crystals in direct contact with the earth for as long as you feel is necessary. Then, thank Mother Earth and its energies with authentic words spoken from your heart. Gather up your crystals and return them to their current home.

4 – ORGONE DEVICES

As well as using orgone devices to clear energies from your crystals, orgone devices can also be used to charge them.

Place an orgone device near or touching the crystals you intend to charge. Using your intuition and intentions, ask that the crystals be charged with whatever energies you desire or are currently working with. Maybe you need help with protection, grounding, forgiveness, connecting to your higher self, or spirit guides, or for cultivating a space of love.

OTHER THINGS TO DO WITH CRYSTALS

PLACE CRYSTALS ON THE CHAKRAS

Begin by selecting and acquiring a crystal for each of the seven chakras of the body. There are specific crystals that resonate and benefit each chakra in the body, and this information is easy to obtain at a crystal shop, in books on crystals, and online.

With your collection of crystals for each chakra, simply lay down and place each crystal on the corresponding chakra. You can place a crystal on just one specific chakra, or all seven of the body. Take at least three deep breaths and relax into an open, calm state. Focus your thoughts and intentions on the crystals clearing, activating, and spinning your chakras. Stay laying down with the crystals for at least ten minutes, or as long as you feel called to do it for.

THIS PRACTICE CAN ENHANCE:

- The healing and body work being done simultaneously
- The activation of the chakras
- The clearing of stagnant energies
- A state of harmonious vibrations

CRYSTAL GRIDS

Crystal grids offer an opportunity to deepen your practice and relationship with crystals by enhancing the combined energies of the crystals. The combination of the crystal's energies, the sacred geometric shape, and the intentions behind the creation make crystal grids extremely powerful and potent.

The geometric shape you choose will determine the number of crystals you will need to complete the shape. For beginners, it is a good idea to start with a simple, basic geometric shape, such as a triangle, circle, square, or spiral. As you get more comfortable with making crystal grids, you can try some of the more intricate geometric shapes. Find elaborate geometric shapes online, or in books on crystal grids. Then, all you have to do is place the crystals on top of the image at the specific points of the geometric shape. Each sacred geometric shape helps amplify certain qualities and attributes.

SOME EXAMPLES ARE:

- TRIANGLE—for promoting simplicity and structure in your life
- CIRCLE—for promoting courage, strength, and protection
- SQUARE—for establishing and maintaining boundaries
- SPIRAL—for expanding and connecting consciousness up into the higher realms

To set intentions for the creation of a crystal grid, get a clear and focused idea of what you would like to activate, enhance or stimulate in your life. Maybe you are searching for guidance, strength, healing, connection, love, relaxation, or better sleep. Find a sacred geometric symbol that will help you with your chosen intentions.

For the crystals, you can use one type or have a variety of crystals. They can be smaller, tumbled crystals, which are inexpensive to acquire. It is beneficial to have at least one clear quartz point crystal as it will assist in directing and sending out the energies and intentions involved during the process.

To get started, gather crystals and choose a sacred geometric shape depending on what sorts of energies you want to magnify. Get clear on the intentions you have for the grid you will create. Choose a safe and convenient place to set up your crystal grid, such as in your living room on a table, under your bed, near a meditation space, or on a kitchen counter. The space you choose could depend on how long you are planning on leaving it set up. Another good idea might be to set up your crystal grid on a moveable platform, making it convenient to move the grid around.

With all materials gathered, geometric shape chosen, intentions set, and the place of set up determined, you are ready to build your crystal grid. After creating the crystal grid, it is important to activate it with authentic, heart-felt words focused on your intended outcome. Let your intuition guide you in this process.

You can leave your crystal grid set up for as long as you feel is appropriate: it can be a little time as just a few hours or as many as several weeks. You could meditate with the crystal grid or when you pass by it, you could remember and focus on the intentions you set out when you created it.

Another great idea is to add other natural elements to your crystal grid. It does not just have to be crystals, as other natural elements also hold beautiful energies of the earth and sky. You could use a special rock, beach glass, shells, pieces of wood, flowers, plants, blades of grass, sand, or dirt.

FINAL THOUGHTS...

Crystals can offer us much needed support in these highly charged times. They *want* to help and be of service to you! Crystals also love to be given away. Give them as gifts to family and friends. Gift yourself. And most importantly, give crystals away to strangers! Give them to people you meet throughout your day... the store clerk, the bank teller, the bus driver, the waitress, or the homeless person you pass on the street. I even like to leave them on park benches or other public spaces for people to find. It will not cost you a lot of money, but it will bring love, gratitude, and a spark of happiness to the receiver. It is easy to find inexpensive crystals.

Remember to respect and cherish your crystals; they appreciate your energy too! Show them love and appreciation, and take care of them. Use them to assist you in aspects of your life that you may be struggling with, but remember not to get too attached to them. Sometimes your time together is short, and other times you may have them for decades. The help that they are giving you might come to an end, or you may out-grow each other. Be prepared for this, and when it is time for them to move on, let them go with love and gratitude.

CHAPTER 7

SPIRIT GUIDES

Chapter 7
SPIRIT GUIDES

As we are currently on the physical plane of the 3rd dimension of consciousness in our human bodies, our senses are extremely limited. This is part of the plan, and it enables us to focus on this one experience in the present moment of time. If we could fully see everything that is truly going on, it would make this 3rd dimensional experience very difficult. Imagine trying to drive a vehicle and being able to see all realms and dimensions of consciousness . . . we would very likely crash.

Our senses are mostly limited to sight, sound, taste, smell, and touch. With these senses, we interpret and experience the world around us. We take in information that creates our own personal reality. Senses can be heightened or diminished depending on our different lifestyles, the way we treat our bodies, and how connected we are to ourselves, others, and the natural world around us.

> *We **see** the vibrant colours that surround us*
> *We **hear** the vibrations of sound*
> *We **smell** the fragrances floating in the air*
> *We **taste** the creations of nourishment*
> *We **feel** and **sense** that which is inside and out*
>
> *But that is not all there is . . .*
> *So much more is present and occurring*
> *We just currently lack the ability to see everything*

There exists multiple dimensions of consciousness beyond our current span of awareness, and we will have opportunities to gain awareness and rise to them. At this moment of time, however, we are exactly where we are meant to be. *Why?* Because we are here.

That being said, everyone does have some access to all dimensions because although we are in a dimension of separation and duality, ultimately we are one and connected on a deeper level. This connection is a vast, complex collective consciousness.

One of the ways we can access the higher dimensions of consciousness and universal knowledge, is through our spirit guides and the divine Universe itself. Inside each sacred one of us exists extraordinary senses and abilities we can remember, relearn, and reconnect with.

The further we reconnect with our inner knowing, our *divine souls*—when all labels, roles, accomplishments, characters (all ego) are stripped away—the more we can reconnect with what lies beyond the veil of illusion, our higher self, and spirit guides.

The more open-hearted, open-minded, and perceptive we are, the more that communication with higher dimensions of consciousness will open up. From this space of openness and receptiveness, we are vibrating at a higher frequency, which makes us more attuned to the consciousness at higher dimensions.

When we begin to accept the truth that we are all ultimately connected, we also begin to realize that we are all a part of the divine Universe. Everything is created from this divine Universe (God, Source, Allah, etc.), and thus, each one of us contains a speck of its divine energy. Once we can gain this awareness of just how special, unique, and powerful we all are, many of our hidden psychic abilities will be able to shine through and be used to create a pristine kingdom right here on the earthly plane for everyone.

Reconnecting and remembering does not happen overnight; it is a slower, intimate unfolding of layers. Communicating with our spirit guides directly can take some time as we build a deeper relationship with ourselves and the natural world that surrounds us. Although our spirit guides are always with us, many of us are not fully conscious of their presence. They are ever-present, constantly offering support, healing, guidance, and unconditional love. Our spirit guides and the divine Universe communicate with us through songs, books, other people, thoughts, impulses, feelings, dreams, numbers, and many other ways. There are already many people with the ability to even see and hear their spirit guides directly.

We all subconsciously know of this connection with our spirit guides, and that is why we call out their names when we are desperate, in deep emotional or physical pain, dying, depressed, lost, or in a state of overwhelming fear. One of the most popular spirit guide that people across the globe call upon, is Jesus of Nazareth. People call out his name in times of great need even if they follow no religion or even believe in him. Still, they call out his name. Every single time his name is called, he is there with them.

> *Our spirit guides*
> *Ever-present benevolent beings*
> *Genuine lifelong companions*
> *Never pass judgment*
> *Only celebrate our deeds*
> *Support us during hardships*
> *Our escorts into higher dimensions of consciousness*

There are countless numbers of different spirit guides currently working with and guiding all the people of this planet. They are all unique and have different strengths, abilities, and purposes. Some spirit guides work with us for short periods of our journeys, and others may be with us for the entirety of this human experience. Many have worked with us in other lifetimes. It is their utmost pleasure to serve us as we walk this journey of the human experience. In order to achieve deeper connections, though, we must be open to them and ask for their help as spirit guides cannot infringe on our *free will*.

There exist cosmic rules of engagement for spirit guides that nothing can influence humans on the 3rd dimension of consciousness against their free will. They can offer us all the support, guidance, healing, and love, but it is up to us whether the connection is made and the messages are received or not. Therefore, if we desire their connection, we must ask and accept it from our own free will. Use your intuition to steer toward those that resonate with you and your own personal experiences and desires. Always ask to be connected with spirit guides of a high vibrational, loving heart-space.

Connecting and working with your spirit guides is a very personal relationship and should come from a space of mutual respect. Although spirit guides are deeply connected to the divine Universe, are full of knowledge and experience, are masters of their psychic abilities and reside on a higher level of existence, they **do not** want to be worshipped. Through their work with us, spirit guides are attempting to show us that we are just like them: we are one and the same and all a part of the divine Universe. We are capable of everything they are capable of, we are just in a state of remembering and reconnecting to that knowledge. Our spirit guides are always at hand during this dissolving of the veil of illusion and the awakening process.

EXAMPLES OF SPIRIT GUIDES:

- Your ancestors
- Angels
- Archangels
- Ascended Masters
- Animal spirits
- Elementals
- Cosmic Beings from other planets and galaxies
- Departed religious icons

BENEFITS OF WORKING WITH SPIRIT GUIDES:

- Support when feeling alone, lost, depressed, or fearful
- Guidance when faced with hard decisions

- LOVE
- Wisdom to perceive a bigger picture or different perspectives
- Shared knowledge gained from vast experience
- Comfort in times of emotional or physical pain
- Relief from emotional and physical pain
- Psychic surgery
- Emotional and physical healing
- DNA activations
- Understanding of personal and global karma
- An ever-attentive listener
- Companionship

HOW TO CALL UPON YOUR SPIRIT GUIDES:

Working with your spirit guides is an extremely personal connection. There really is no wrong way to do it, though it should always be done with mutual respect and come from a space of love. Spirit guides communicate through many different ways, such as through music, numbers, voices inside your head, bright sparkly light, warm tingles, and so many more ways. As you develop and grow your relationships with spirit guides, you will find your own way of communicating.

Here is an example of how you could start:

- Take some deep breaths
- If you know their name, call upon them using their proper name
- Otherwise, simply call upon spirit guides from the 5D unity consciousness or higher
- Say something such as:

  "Of my own free will, I call upon my spirit guides of a high vibrational loving heart-space. Please be with me now"

- Ask for the support you need, or pose questions you have
- Ask for healing energy or comfort and love
- Ask for whatever you need
- You can ask with your voice, silently inside your head, or write it down
- At first, there may seem to be no response. This is very normal, as our senses are overloaded and we have to slow down, quiet our minds, and get into our heart space

- Know that your spirit guides *are* there, even if you cannot sense them
- The more you call upon them and open yourself up to their replies, the more the connection will come
- This connection cannot be rushed
- Give yourself plenty of time to just be quiet, open, and aware
- Have no expectations or attachment to the outcome
- Only you and your spirit guides know *how* to communicate with each other
- In your stillness, be aware of your feelings, body and surroundings
- When you are finished, *always thank your spirit guides*
- Watch for synchronicities in your life that may be your spirit guides responding
- Build a deep relationship of mutual trust and respect from a space of love and truth

OTHER WAYS OF CONNECTING WITH SPIRIT GUIDES:

- Freewriting
- Meditating
- Tarot cards
- Pendulums
- Crystals
- Through psychics, mediums, or highly connected and conscious people

DAILY RESET

Every time we go to sleep, there is a reset. As a planet of free will, nothing can directly or indirectly work with us unless we agree to it, either subconsciously or consciously. We need to re-establish a connection daily, if we so desire.

You can connect to your spirit guides easily and quickly, by just calling their name out loud or thinking about them. Adding some requests and intentions to the process can be very helpful, however. You could say something such as:

> *"Of my own free will, I call upon/connect with my higher self, ascended masters, archangels, beings from the 5th dimension or higher. Work through me, love through me, speak through me, act through me, guide me, support me, and help clear any energies from all my bodies that are not mine. And so it is."*

FINAL THOUGHTS...

For me, spirit guides have been like having a best friend that is ever-present and always supportive. At this point of my journey, I do not see or hear them directly. Instead, I *feel* them and have thoughts come to me. My spirit guides communicate to me through my thoughts, intuition, numbers, music, books, other people, and beautiful, unexplainable synchronicities. Each spirit guide has their own way of connecting with me, but when I directly call upon one of them, I feel their energy instantly surround me. It is like a warming sensation around and inside my body. With some spirit guides, I will have thoughts enter my mind that offer new ideas and perspectives or just feelings of comfort, support, and love. With others, I get no immediate response, but later messages will come through in a song, a chance meeting, or numbers. I then have to consciously put the pieces of the message together for myself.

I have always been strongly drawn to archangels, elementals, Buddha and beings from other planets, such as the Arcturians and the Pleiadians. Over the past ten years or so, I have been working closely with Jesus, Mary Magdalene, and Mother Mary. I have never followed religious dogmas; instead, I always felt a deep and direct spiritual connection with nature and the divine Universe. It never made sense to me that I needed anyone to connect me to that which I come from and am already a part of.

Ultimately, the connection between you and your spirit guides is very personal and does not require anyone else to make this connection for you. That being said, there are highly conscious people who are very connected and can offer guidance and advice based off of their own experiences. You are a speck of the divine Universe and this can never be taken away or broken. We just needed to remember and re-establish our connection so we can open up the lines of communication.

CHAPTER 8

HEALING MODALITIES

Chapter 8
HEALING MODALITIES

Although each and every one of us is a powerful healer, many of us do not remember our skills and abilities. Part of our journey involves remembering the forgotten knowledge of these natural skills and abilities, though it may take many years of unfolding.

> *It involves taking our power back*
> *The power we gave away unknowingly*
> *The power we were programmed to forget*
> *It involves re-gaining our personal faith & belief*
> *Faith & belief in ourselves*
> *And re-discovering our connection to the natural world*

Until that time comes, we can make use of the skills and abilities of other people who have already rediscovered some of their natural powers to heal and clear energies. Currently, many people are working in alternative healing techniques and energy work, and it may be beneficial for you to connect with some of them. There also are many ancient books and practices that have been passed down throughout the ages all over the world in various cultures.

> *Always remember . . . you are a healer too!*

To find people who will help with healing energy work, do some research around your local area for in-person sessions, or find many healers who can facilitate and execute sessions at a distance. Research books, ancient writings, and verbal modalities pass down from our ancestors and other cultures of the world. Follow your intuition and feelings, and always be respectful. Let them be your guide in finding people, books or verbal modalities to work with. Always remember that they are just like you, maybe a little more advanced along their personal journey, but just like you. Do not put them on a pedestal; you are also a powerful speck of the infinite divine Universe.

TYPES OF SPIRITUAL HEALERS:

- Shamans
- Light workers
- Energy workers
- Gurus
- Ritual healers
- Earth angels
- Reiki masters

EXAMPLES OF SPIRITUAL HEALING MODALITIES:

- Crystal healing
- Reiki
- Hypnotherapy
- Therapeutic touch
- Electromagnetic therapy
- Ozone therapy
- Neuro-linguistic programming
- Sacred plant medicines
- Traditional Eastern medicines
- Homeopathy
- Ayurveda
- Acupuncture
- Aromatherapy
- Massage
- Reflexology
- Cupping
- Spooning
- Western herbal medicine

When working with an experienced healer in energy work, remember that you ultimately control what is transpiring with your beliefs, thoughts, and ideas. These healers are initially facilitating and activating your own body's natural abilities to heal itself. They are helping to reconnect you to your innate healing abilities.

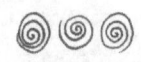

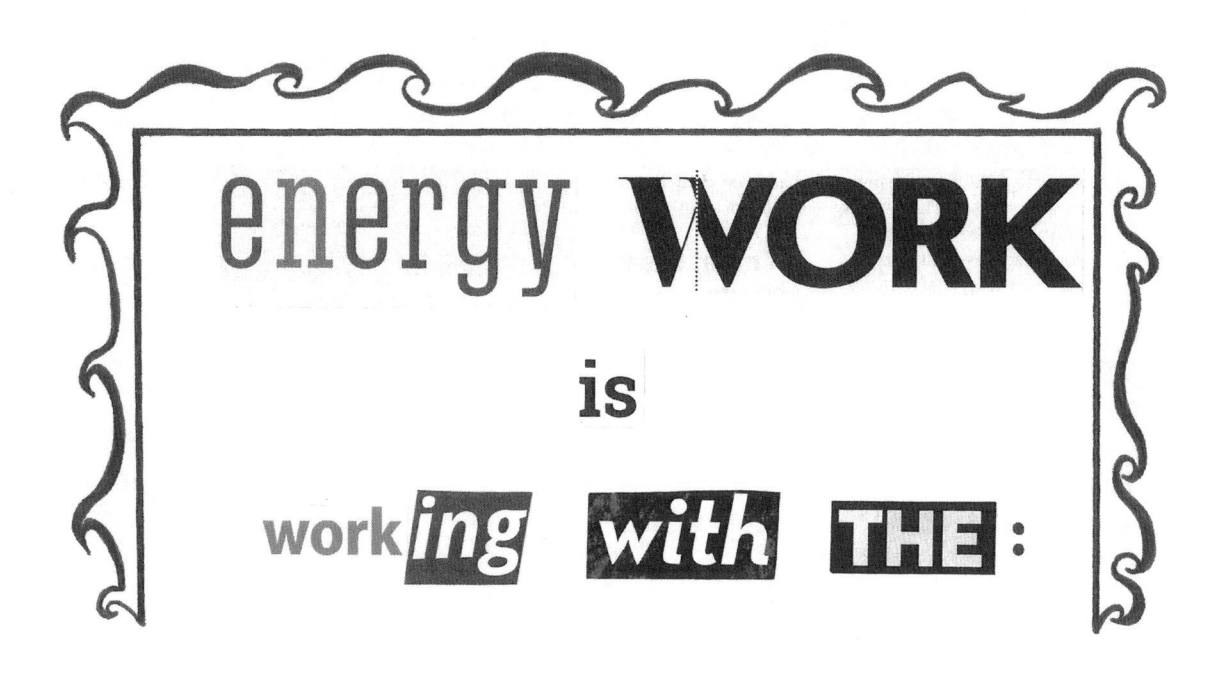

energy WORK

is

working with THE:

- Ⓢ **EMPATHIC Body** Ⓢ
- Ⓢ **ETHERIC Body** Ⓢ
- Ⓢ **Astral body** Ⓢ
- Ⓢ **spiritUal BODY** Ⓢ
- Ⓢ **mental BODY** Ⓢ
- Ⓢ **PHYSICAL body** Ⓢ

NATURE FOR HEALING

Our natural world is full of organic elements to assist and support us along this journey of the human experience. Simply spending time outside in nature can improve and restore your emotional, mental, and physical state of being. Breathing in the fresh air will fill your lungs, brain and body with renewed energy. Watching the clouds or water flowing by will clear the mind and bring a calmness to the body.

TREES

Trees provide us with life-giving oxygen, shade, medicines, food, and are able to clear energy from our emotional and physical bodies. Giant trees, small trees, trees with soft leaves, trees with prickly branches—oh what a variety exists! Trees are immensely powerful and ever present.

PLANTS, HERBS AND FLOWERS

Apart from their beauty and aromatic qualities, plants, herbs, and flowers have numerous medicinal uses. They can help with pain and inflammation; they can clear toxins from the body, heal many illnesses, and so much more. Plants, herbs, and flowers have been used for physical, mental, and emotional healing for thousands of generations by various cultures across the world.

EXAMPLES OF SACRED PLANTS, HERBS AND FLOWERS USED AROUND THE WORLD:

Western Indigenous Cultures

- Tobacco, sweet grass, cedar, sage, diamond willow fungus

Latin American Cultures

- Ayahuasca, cumin, sage, spearmint, aloe vera, chamomile, wormwood

East Indian Cultures

- Garcinia, nagarmusta, neem, horseradish tree, bitter melon, licorice

African Cultures

- Cape aloe, devil's claw, rooibos, hoodia, buchu, kambo

Asian Cultures

- Ginger, ginseng, cinnamon, astragalus, ginkgo biloba

A GUIDE TO THE COLLECTIVE AWAKENING

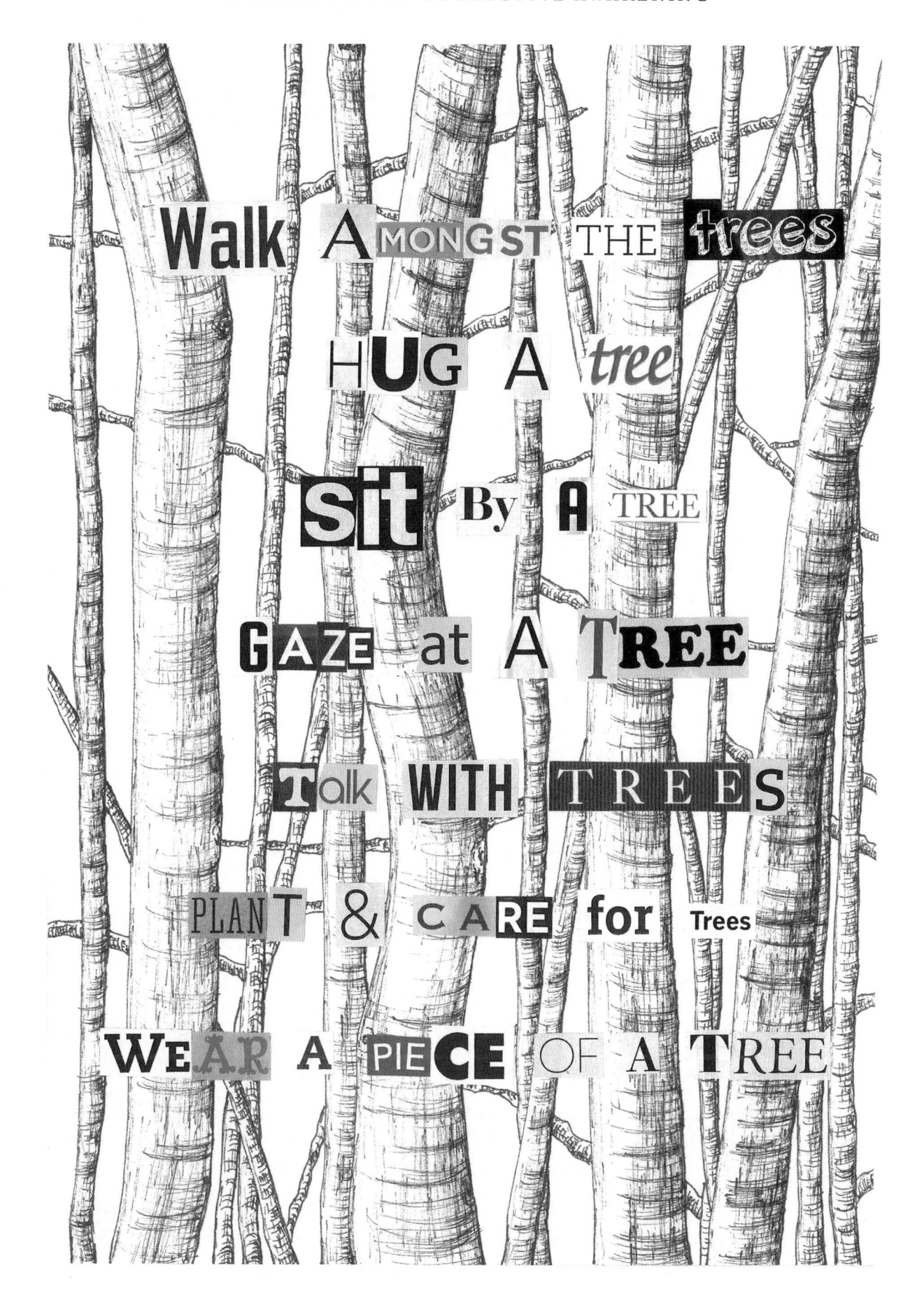

Walk Amongst the trees

Hug A tree

Sit By A tree

Gaze at A Tree

Talk WITH TREES

Plant & Care for Trees

Wear A Piece Of A Tree

AROMATHERAPY

Our sense of smell is a very important way for us to experience and interpret the world around us. For thousands of years, many cultures have known the power of aromatherapy to promote health and well-being, both physically and psychologically.

> *Aromatherapy reaches our **mind**, **body** and **spirit***

Aromatherapy is a profoundly useful tool to utilize during the awakening process. Pleasant and natural scents can comfort in times of emotional or physical discomfort, distract our minds from negative thoughts, aid in relaxation, clear energy, and much more.

There are numerous essential oils available, and each one has its own specific uses and benefits. Based on your personal aliments and desires, do some research to see which essential oils can help. Whether you require emotional support, relief from a physical condition, or assistance with clearing energy, there is an essential oil that can help. There are even essential oils that can clean and boost the body's immune system.

METHODS FOR USING ESSENTIAL OILS:

- Topical application with a carrier oil
- Diffuser or oil burner
- Aromatic spritzer
- Incense sticks or cones
- Candles
- Bath salts, soaps, and bubble bath
- Body creams, lotions, or oils
- Oral ingestion (for some essential oils)
- Breathing in the smell from the bottle

When purchasing essential oils, ensure they are from a reputable source and contain no additives or synthetic ingredients. You want to be sure the plant extracts are pure and processed in a reliable method. Also, before using any essential oils, make sure you are familiar with its proper uses, any safety precautions, therapeutic properties, and proper storage.

Besides using prepared essential oils, the natural world offers an abundance of aromas at no cost. By immersing yourself in nature, you will be surrounded by the many gifts nature has to offer you.

> **The smell of...**
> *Fresh rain, grass, dirt, the ocean, the sea, flowers, herbs, plants, and trees*

NATURAL BODIES OF WATER

In the chapter on water, I discussed many of the benefits and ways to use water in our lives, so I will try not to repeat myself too much. Natural bodies of water are powerful energy movers. Find relief and comfort by being near or in water. Immerse your hands, feet, or entire body in it. Stand at the water's edge and release emotions by screaming, crying to the water, or silently talking about your troubles. The water will clear this energy for you if you so desire and set the intention.

> **Go to...**
> *The sea, the ocean, a river or lake, a stream or creek, a waterfall, or hot spring*

THE SKY

It can be remarkably relaxing and restorative to stare at the sky... the big, open, blue sky, the clouds, the rain, rainbows, snow falling, the stars, the rising or setting of the sun. Opening yourself up to the vastness of the sky above, can fill you with a sense of peaceful calming energy. It may assist your subconscious and conscious awareness to open up to the bigger cosmic journey taking place. Let the sky help take you out of the day-to-day narrow perspective of the human experience.

> *Be like the sky... open, infinite and flowing*

SOUND FOR HEALING

Sound has a remarkably powerful effect on our mind and body. Connected to one of our basic five senses, sound is a way in which we perceive the world around us and interact with it.

At this time in our journeys, sound can be a very useful tool to support the physical and mental bodies. It helps us adapt to the raising of vibrations the world is currently experiencing through the awakening process. Certain sounds may relax and calm us, as well as assist in releasing pent-up emotions in a cathartic way. It may also fill us with energy and stimulate inspiration. Through sounds such as music, we deepen our connection and understanding of people from across the globe. Music can ignite and inspire passion within us. It can even trigger memories from our past, giving us an opportunity to heal and clear unwanted energies from our bodies.

CALMING SOUNDS:

- Water sounds:
  - *Waves*
  - *Rainfall*
  - *Waterfalls*
  - *Flowing rivers*
  - *Babbling brooks*
- Soft music:
  - *Instrumental music*
  - *Spa music*
  - *Meditation music*
  - *Classical music*
  - *432 Hz or 528 Hz music*

- A gentle breeze
- Birds
- Crickets or frogs
- Chakra sounds
- Singing bowls
- Drums
- Digeridoo
- Gentle flutes
- The breath
- Rain-stick
- Throat singing
- Humming/toning

> We find the sound of water so relaxing and comforting
> It reminds us of the sounds we first heard inside our Mother's Womb
> All that being said...
> ***No** sound is also beneficial*
> *In the silence*
> *There is still sound*
> *A gentle hum or buzz*

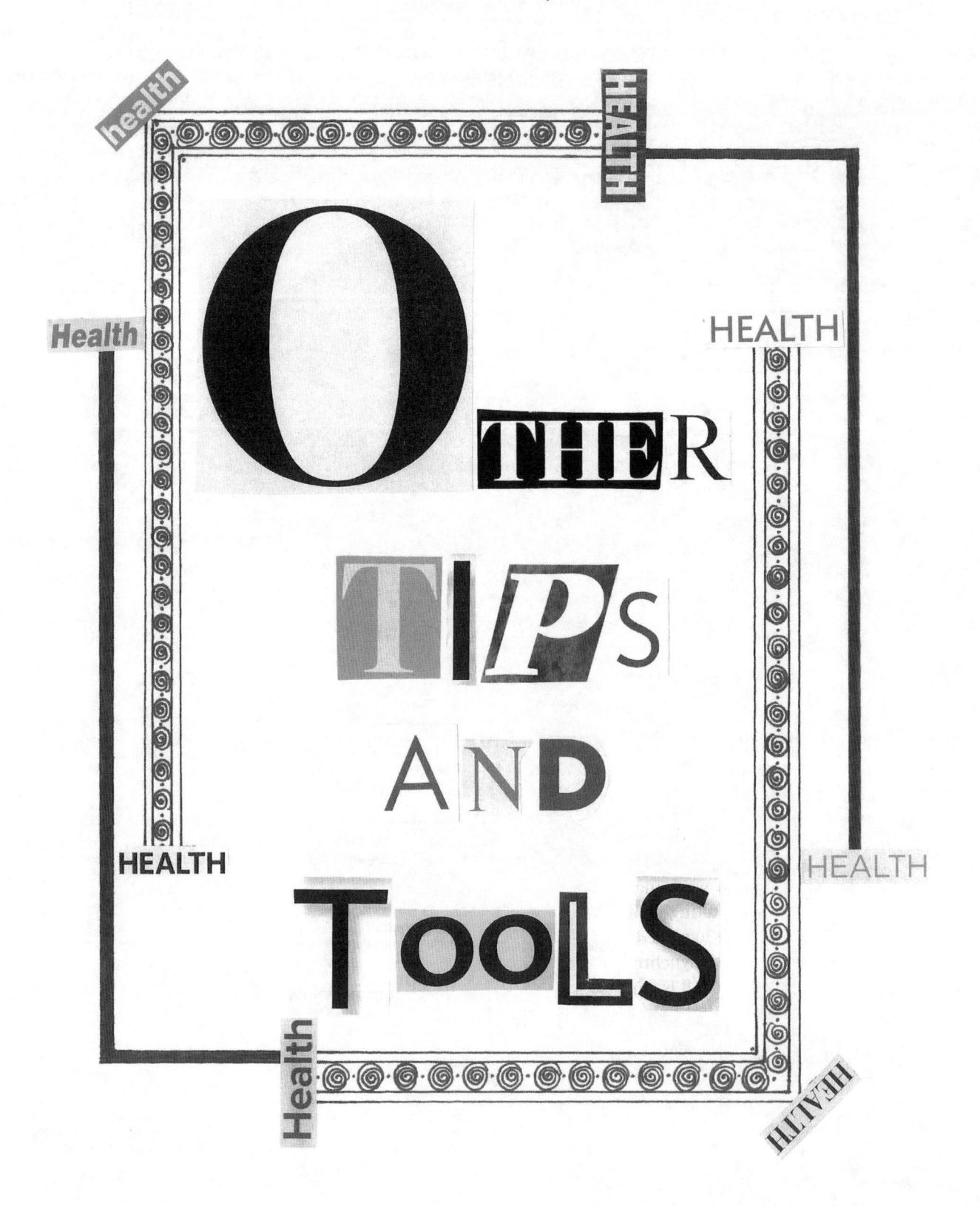

CHAPTER 9

Other Tips and Tools

Chapter 9
OTHER TIPS AND TOOLS

PSYCHIC ABILITIES—OUR DIVINE POWERS

In addition to the five senses of the human body, we are also capable of tapping into and utilizing our sixth sense—our psychic abilities. Regaining the ability to access and employ our divine powers is a significant part of the awakening journey. It is important to reclaim our power, that which we gave away unknowingly and were probably manipulated out of by unseen and unknown forces since the time of our birth.

With the unravelling of our extrasensory perceptions, we will begin to perceive the world with a greater attuned and connected state of knowing and acceptance. Life circumstances can become more of a flow of opportunities and experiences of higher consciousness. Communication lines can open up. We can be reconnected to all the knowledge of the divine Universe and expand from a state of unity consciousness.

Where do we start? . . .

We may already be using some of our psychic abilities and are not even consciously aware of it. In the beginning, these natural abilities are subtle, but if we take time to develop and strengthen them, they will only grow in power.

One of the most common psychic abilities is intuition—that gut feeling we get about people, places, or situations. This is when we just know how things will turn out, or what people will do before they do it. Our intuition offers us guidance along our journey.

> *We must come to a space of trust*
> *Trust and belief in one's self and abilities*
> *We must be open and perceptive to the invisible*
> *The cosmic universal energies in the nonphysical plane*

A good place to start is to get re-acquainted with the knowledge of psychic abilities. Today, many scientifically documented studies of viable examples of people with psychic abilities are available.

Possibly while gathering information, you will discover that some of them are already unravelling within you. Or you may be inspired to practice and build a specific ability that seems to be calling to your attention.

EXAMPLES OF PSYCHIC ABILITIES:

- <u>Astral Projection</u>—the ability of the consciousness and mental body to travel to another place while the physical body remains in the original place

- <u>Clairvoyance</u>—the ability to know, predict, or see beyond the normal range of perception. A deep sense of knowing

- <u>Channelling</u>—the ability to communicate with higher dimensional beings, spirit guides, or people from the past or future

- <u>Telekinesis</u>—the ability to move matter/objects with one's mind

- <u>Levitation</u>—the ability to suspend the physical body by floating or flying in mid air

- <u>Telepathy</u>—the ability to read and know the thoughts and internal dialogue of another person

As my personal intuition has been developing, I have found it extremely helpful to ask for verifiable results. If I can verify something I have an intuition about, it strengthens my belief about my ability, and the more I trust it, the stronger it grows. For example, I will often intuitively know what my husband is thinking about or feeling, and I can ask him to verify if I am right or not.

SELF-LOVE AND SELF-CARE

As we collectively make our way to a higher level of conscious awareness and, simultaneously, a loving, harmonious planet, it is important to remember that we first need to focus on *ourselves*. All the positive changes in the world will start inside each one of us. It is up to each individual to do their own personal work. No one can fix you, and you cannot fix anyone else either. We can temporarily help each other and offer love and support, but to have true healing and wisdom, it must come from within.

> *We must remember what we truly are:*
> **_Infinite and eternal divine beings of light_**
> *We are powerful, intelligent, creative, adaptable, and loving beings*
> *The human spirit achieves inspiring accomplishments and survives staggering hardships*
> *So . . .*
> *We need to have true unconditional love and acceptance of ourselves*
> **_All_** *of ourselves*
> *The beautiful parts and the parts we deem ugly*
> *Through love we can heal all*
> *Through love we can change everything*
> *But it all starts with authentic love of one's self*

WAYS OF CULTIVATING SELF-LOVE AND SELF-CARE:

- Listen to your body's needs
- Try to ignore all negative self-talk—Replace it with positive self-talk
- Be grateful for what you do have
- Eat healthy *real* food prepared with love and care
- Drink *real* live water
- Express your emotions in healthy ways
- Follow your dreams
- Treat yourself to special gifts
- Spend time in nature
- Talk to your body with loving words of gratitude
- Every day, tell yourself "I love you"
- Write a list of your positive qualities and traits
- Surround yourself with people who love and respect you
- Sit quietly with yourself and just breathe
- Give your body adequate sleep
- Make time in your day for moments of stillness

- Move the body = move energy
  - Take walks in nature
  - Try yoga, Qigong, Tai Chi
  - Go for a swim or a bike ride
  - Do some gardening
  - Play a game with children outside
  - Stretch the body

GRATITUDE

Gratitude is a powerful tool for attracting abundance in our lives. The more we are grateful for, the more there will be to be grateful for. When we are in a state of gratitude, we are sending the divine Universe the message that we are ready for more things to be grateful for. Whatever we focus on is what we are attracting and manifesting into our lives. Being in a state of gratitude raises our vibration, lifts our spirits, and fills us with love and appreciation in the present moment. It can help to shift our focus or thoughts if we feel stuck on a downward spiral of pain or victimhood.

Being in a state of gratitude does not mean we avoid or ignore our current situation and problems, however. The issues in our lives exist; they are happening. But being in a state of gratitude gives us an opportunity to shift our focus to what we *do* have, however small that may be. Through gratitude, we open a space in our present awareness of the positive aspects of our current circumstances, which in turn can help us with the negative aspects.

It truly is the little things that matter most. We do not need extravagant objects or remarkable accomplishments to be grateful. It could be something as simple as being thankful for the sunshine, a smile from a stranger, a healthy meal, or a refreshing glass of clean water. Often, there are many things in our daily lives that we take for granted, but a closer look may help us see just how blessed we already are.

We have to start somewhere, so make it easy and think about the simple things already present. Do you have food, water, shelter, clothes, amenities, a hot shower, a bed, your physical and mental health? What about loved ones, like family, children and friends? Do you have farmers growing your food and truck drivers delivering all the products you buy? What about doctors and nurses that assist with your health, or teachers educating you or your children? Or nonphysical things, such as love, safely, comfort, adequate rest, laughter, and joy?

Even if you can only think of a few things to be grateful for, focus all your attention of them. Let all other thoughts fall away for a while. Become aware of all your five senses. Focus on what you are grateful for and ponder what it looks, smells, and sounds like, as well as how it feels to the touch, and—if it applies—how it tastes. Experience and deeply remember the things you are grateful for from various angles and perspectives to increase your focus.

WAYS TO CULTIVATE GRATITUDE:

- Write in a gratitude journal—list five things you are grateful for every day
- Upon waking, spend a few minutes thinking of things you are grateful for
- Before falling asleep, spend a few minutes thinking of things you are grateful for
- Say thank you to everything and everyone throughout your day
- Help those less fortunate
- Let the people in your life know how grateful you are for them and the things they do
- Meditate with mantras of gratitude
- Learn about how other people live around the world
- Let go of comparing anything to everything

GROUNDING

Grounding, also known as "earthing," is similar to some meditation techniques. Both practices are about getting us out of our thinking mind and returning our focus to the physical body and our surroundings, returning to the present moment.

Grounding helps reconnect us to the energies of the Earth and nature. It can also help relieve stress, anxiety, and feelings of being overwhelmed and disconnected. By making direct contact with Mother Earth, unwanted energies can be drained out of your physical, emotional, and mental bodies.

WAYS TO GROUND:

- **Make physical contact with Mother Earth**
  - Walk barefoot on the grass, dirt, sand, etc.

- Touch a tree with your bare hands
- Touch your hands to the earth—water, sand, grass, dirt, etc.
- Immerse your hands or whole body in water
- **Focus on things around you with your five senses**
  - What do you **hear**?
  - What do you **see**?
  - What do you **smell**?
  - What can you **touch**?
  - What can you **taste**?
- **Hold or be near grounding crystals**
  - Jet, obsidian, black tourmaline, Apache tears, hematite, jade, jasper and agate

CUTTING CORDS

At this time on the planet, many people have forgotten how to naturally connect with the life-force energy in and all around us. This life-force energy emanates from the divine Universe, the sun, and from within all living forms. Like food, this life-force energy provides us with power and substance to maintain optimum health and balance in our lives. Unfortunately, the lack of this natural knowledge leaves people feeling disconnected, unstable, drained, and empty. This then leads to people taking energy from each other in order to fill the essential life-force energy absent in their lives. This is how energetic cords are created between people. A link is created that can receive or extract life-force energy from either side.

In the current conditions of life in the 3rd dimension of consciousness, it can sometimes be helpful to have energetic cords linked to another person. The bond between a parent and a child is a great example of this. The child, for healthy emotional development to occur, requires support and draws on the parents for ample amounts of emotional support. The parents, in turn, receive energy from the joy of helping their child thrive and grow.

When we are sending thoughts, intentions, or prayers out into the world for someone, we are sending them energetic cords of our life-force energy. Sometimes it is loving and supportive energy, but it can also be hateful and jealous energy.

Some people may already be aware of the exchange of life-force energy between themselves and others. The awareness of this energy exchange provides a beneficial perspective on how to look after your own energy field (your aura) and, if possible, help others with theirs. It is very important, and helpful, to be in touch with the energetic cords you may have established with people and be able to manage the exchange in a balanced and health way. Sometimes we get overwhelmed or depleted in life-force energy, and we need to focus solely on ourselves. At these times, it is extremely helpful to know how to cut energy cords and thus, be with your own energy.

Unfortunately, there are people who are deeply disconnected with themselves and the divine Universe. They have scarcely experienced true, unconditional love, support, or compassion in their lives. This would leave anyone to feel alone, desperate, and possibly full of envy, entitlement, and a focus on revenge. Sadly, most of these people become "energy vampires" and attempt to suck the life-force energy out of others because they lack their own connection. They can manipulate people into creating the cord for them, or they can just establish it for themselves.

Many of us are remembering how to tap into our innate connection to the divine Universe, where life-force energy is unlimited for all. But, until we have mastered the eternal divine connection, it is important to take care of, maintain, and strengthen our own energy fields (our aura). Learning how to cut energy cords that are no longer serving our highest interest, but are instead draining our life-force energy, is an extremely helpful skill. It is possible to unhook unwanted connections to others easily and quickly. By using our imagination to visualize the invisible energy cords, and even asking for help from our spirit guides or higher self, we can disconnect with connections that are no longer in our best interest.

CUTTING ENERGY CORDS:

- Take some deep breaths and clear your mind
- Initially, it helps to close your eyes while attempting to use your imagination
- Visualize, in your mind's eye, your energy field (your aura)
    - What colour is it?
    - How close is it to your physical body?
- Now, visualize the cords of energy coming out of your energy field
    - Imagine what they look like: their characteristics
    - Do they have colour? How thin or thick are they?
    - See these cords stretch out far into the distance, till they disappear out of sight
- Either call upon your spirit guides or your higher self to assist you
    - Through your own free will and intentions, ask for help to cut all cords
- Visualize a tool for cutting and grasp it tightly with confidence

- You could use a small knife, a sword, scissors, wire cutters, etc.
- Either imagine yourself swinging your tool around your body and cutting the cords
    - Or actually swing your arms and imaginary tool around your body
- Visualize the cords being severed and the links being cut
    - This could be done slowly, focusing on one cord at a time
    - Or in a fast flurry of movement, all cords could be disconnected
    - Some cords will cut easily
    - While other cords will require several strong swings
- Visualize yourself grasping the end of the severed cord just disconnected from you
    - Seal the end with intentions of love and support
    - Then send it back to where it came from
- Visualize the area on your energy field where the cord was severed
    - Seal this area with intentions of love and resilience
- Take some deep breaths
- Hold your focus and attention on your energy field for a moment
    - Visualize, once again, your powerful energy field
    - See the wholeness of your aura
    - Set some intentions of strength, completeness and adaptability
- Thank your spirit guides and your higher self for their help and support

The technique of cutting the cords can be done anywhere and will take less than a minute to do. It can be easily modified to fit with your own intuitive ideas, which may come up as you become more comfortable and used to performing this technique.

> *Make it your own—follow your intuition*
> *See what you see, move how you move*
> *Say the words that feel right for you*

When I am cutting my own energy cords, I generally call upon Archangel Michael to help and support me through the process. Archangel Michael is usually depicted holding a sword and is known for his strength and protection. This is why Archangel Michael is often the main spirit guide associated with cord cutting.

Sometimes, I will just visualize myself sitting or standing in front of Archangel Michael and asking him to help me cut and clear all the cords attached to my energy field. I will imagine him swinging his sword around my entire circumference, and watch as the cords fall away. Other times, I will visualize myself holding a sword in my hands and actually wave my arms around myself, pretending to cut the cords. Either way, I always seal both sides of the severed link with love and send the energy back to its original source.

Some of the energy cords that have attached to me have been extremely strong, and it required several hacks to sever the connection. In one instance, I was cutting cords attached to a past sexual partner (my daughter's biological father). As I motioned to sever the cords connected to my uterus coming from him, I felt a quick sharp pain from within my uterus. Luckily, this hasn't happened again. Mostly, cutting cords is fast, painless, and simple to do, and it significantly increases the accumulation of your own natural energy.

Depending on my energy level, I might not cut all the cords. When I feel an intuitive impulse to clear my energy field, a lot of the time I will cut all cords except the ones linking my husband and my daughter to me. If I am feeling overwhelmed and depleted, I will clear all cords.

There is a constant ebb and flow of the energy we share: with each other and everything around us. Since, on a higher level of consciousness, we are all one and the same, we also share the life-force energy inside us. We have the power to spread the vibrational energy of our love out across galaxies, but we can also send the opposite out. So, when you are in need of reclaiming your life-force energy or are in need of some extra self-care, try the process of cutting cords. Follow your own intuition for when and how often to cut cords. As always, do it with love.

CHAPter 10

ART FOR HEALING

Chapter 10
ART FOR HEALING

For as long as I can remember, I have used creativity in my life to express my thoughts, ideas, emotions, feelings, dreams, and so much more. I was always drawn to create something with my hands. It was like a pen or scissors or a part of nature was an extension of me and helped express what was going on inside my mind and body. It soothed me and brought a release I did not fully understand at the time . . . I just felt compelled to do it.

I *love* art! I love to look at and learn about art. From a young age, I had a deep appreciation for all types of art, even the art of nature. Later in life, I finally had the confidence to attend art school and embrace the career of a full-time professional artist. First, I had to overcome the strong opinion of most people around me who thought people could not make art for a living. I also knew that if I wanted to be my best, I had to learn and understand what was done before me. Most art is a conversation . . . it helps to know the language if you want to fully grasp what is being said. Because of our unity consciousness, throughout history many artists have created similar things, though they were worlds apart at the time.

I know about the power of art—*the power of expression*—and the release that can come when creating. I think that through my creations, I have learned more and more about my true self, my abilities, and my purpose. Many times, it was not about a final product, but rather about the creative process. My healing or energy release didn't come from the finished piece of art I had created. It came from the actual process I went through during the creation. It was through the intense slapping of a brush or the hard pressured scrapes of a palette knife that I felt release and relief.

I would love to share this process of healing and release that can occur during the creative process. With my bit of knowledge of, and training in the art world, I hope to facilitate an opportunity for you to discover, or deepen, the healing powers of the creative process. Perhaps this can be a new process that will help you surrender, open up, and truly face what is stirring within you.

Before I walk you through the art projects I put together, I want to share with you some thoughts on art, artists, and the creative process.

CReaTION = RELEASE OF energy & EMOtions

WAYS TO EXPRESS YOURSELF CREATIVELY:

- Painting
- Drawing
- Sculpting
- Photography
- Printmaking
- Earth art
- Performance art
- Digital art
- Redecorating a room
- Designing clothes
- Playing an instrument
- Theater performance
- Costume making
- Making cards or bookmarks
- Making a movie or short video
- Building a sand castle
- Writing in a journal
- Writing poetry or comedy
- Writing fiction or non-fiction
- Writing a children's book
- Writing a song
- Writing a play or graphic novel
- Calligraphy
- Colouring books
- Doodling
- Building a model
- Knitting/crocheting
- Gardening
- Cooking/baking
- Singing
- Dancing
- Making spiral designs out of rocks

ART FOR:

Healing Letting go
Expression Recording history
Emotional release Storytelling
Processing Sharing
Understanding Awareness
Receiving Love
Meditation Fun/Joy
Relaxation
Focus—*strengthen your attention span and patience*

The benefits of the creative process have long been known and used by many who walked the planet before us. A lot of what we know about history comes from the art that was produced at the time. Art has documented many grand and terrible experiences of the human race, though many of the viewpoints responsible for the creation of historical reports are extremely biased.

Art brings people together; it helps people express their experiences and viewpoints in a way that others can understand, relate to, and sympathize with. Art inspires people to strive for beauty, expression, independence, and connection.

Creating art offers a safe process where people can express deep hurts, global tragedies, and personal strife. Many times, tears and words fall on deaf ears—others just cannot grasp, fathom, or understand what happened and how it may have affected someone. Through art, experiences may be revealed in a form that reaches deeper inside a person's heart, consciousness, and subconsciousness. Art inspires one to relate and gain a deeper understanding of the suffering of another. This deeper understanding may lead to true healing, release, and reconciliation and further help prevent the same horrors from repeating in the future.

If we can truly empathize with another's pain and suffering, it has the potential to change outdated and wrong beliefs that are harming so many innocent people. With the release of old thoughts, connections can be made between people of different races, religions, lifestyles, sexual orientation, and so on.

Art is experienced by the viewer in a deeply personal and secluded space—*their mind and body*. Initially, a person experiences art, and their personal reactions to it, with no outside judgments, opinions, or critiques. This may lead to and encourage independent, critical thought.

The viewing of art is so very subjective. The viewer brings with them all of their life experiences, beliefs, ideas, opinions, circumstances, and even their ability to see colour. All of this impacts the way art is seen. This makes one person's view of art completely different from another person's. When looking at a piece of art, such as a painting, one might see beauty while another sees ugliness. With the ability of art to inspire emotion, one person could be filled with sadness and another filled with rage. There is no one way to see or feel about art. There is no right or wrong type of observation; it is simply the reactions and opinions of the viewer.

When Viewing Art, Try to be in a State of...

Openess	Respect
Patience	Reflection
Acceptance	Witness
Acknowledgement	Reverence
Understanding	Empathy
Forgiveness	Sympathy
Appreciation	Connection
Admiration	

Art may also help us express and process our own past or present traumas and emotions. With intentions, a little planning, and a willingness to try, anyone can use the creative process to help deal with difficult life circumstances and facilitate the release of unwanted energies.

We are all creative, in some way or another. Being human, we are constantly involved with the very creation of our collective reality, our Mother Earth, and our own lives—though not always from a place of consciousness and direction.

PROFESSIONAL OR BEGINNER? IT DOESN'T MATTER

Art is not only created by professional, trained, and skilled artists. Art requires no perfection, and it does not have to produce a final product. Art can completely lack any meaning, logic, or purpose. It can be all about the *process*, the act of making, the act of looking, and the act of movement. It may also be about the emotions we are feeling and want to express in a physical form, like a painting or clay sculpture. The possibilities are endless, if you have the willingness to try.

Try not to get stuck on the fact that you can't do something well before even giving yourself the time to develop the basic skills to do it. There doesn't have to be any sort of judgment or expectations. It can solely be about the act of creating—going through the motions.

JENNA WALKER

COMMON THOUGHTS THAT MAY ARISE:

"I'm not an artist"
"I can't make art"
"I don't have any artistic skills"
"I don't know where to begin"
"I don't have any supplies"
"I don't even know what to create"

> *Let all of that go*
> *So much of the creative process*
> *Involves:*
> **<u>Looking</u>**
> *Really seeing*
> *Deciphering with the senses*
> *Analysing with the heart and mind*
> *Breaking down the steps*
> *Doing the actual work*
> *Making mistakes*
> *Adapting and adjusting*
> *Embracing the results*

Genuinely taking the time to visually examine works of art can further develop your understanding and appreciation of it. By learning about the history of how the piece of artwork was made, what materials were used, the time period it was made in, and who made it, the viewing experience of a piece of art can be enhanced. Examining various styles from all over the world and from different time periods may help us discover what we strongly admire and greatly dislike. I think understanding art helps us better understand ourselves and humanity as a whole. Art can inspire us, make us sad with deep empathy, and make us understand something on a deeper level. Art can fill us with rage and disgust, or it can do nothing at all. Certain things speak to certain people. The versatility of art is a gift in itself.

Research is a very useful and eye-opening tool that can broaden perspectives and assist in opening viewpoints to other experiences being had by fellow humans. It can also ignite creativity and help generate new ideas you may want to pursue. Try exposing yourself to all sorts of art—professional art, non-professional art, and everything in between.

WAYS TO VIEW AND EXPERIENCE ART:

- Galleries
- Museums
- Architecture
- Libraries
- Cathedrals/churches
- Gardens
- Books
- Children's books
- Graphic novels
- Magazines
- The internet
- Movies
- Documentaries
- Music videos
- Theater/plays
- Operas/concerts
- Dance performances
- Fashion/clothing design
- Interior/exterior design
- Automobile design
- Furniture design
- Murals
- Street art
- Graffiti

JENNA WALKER

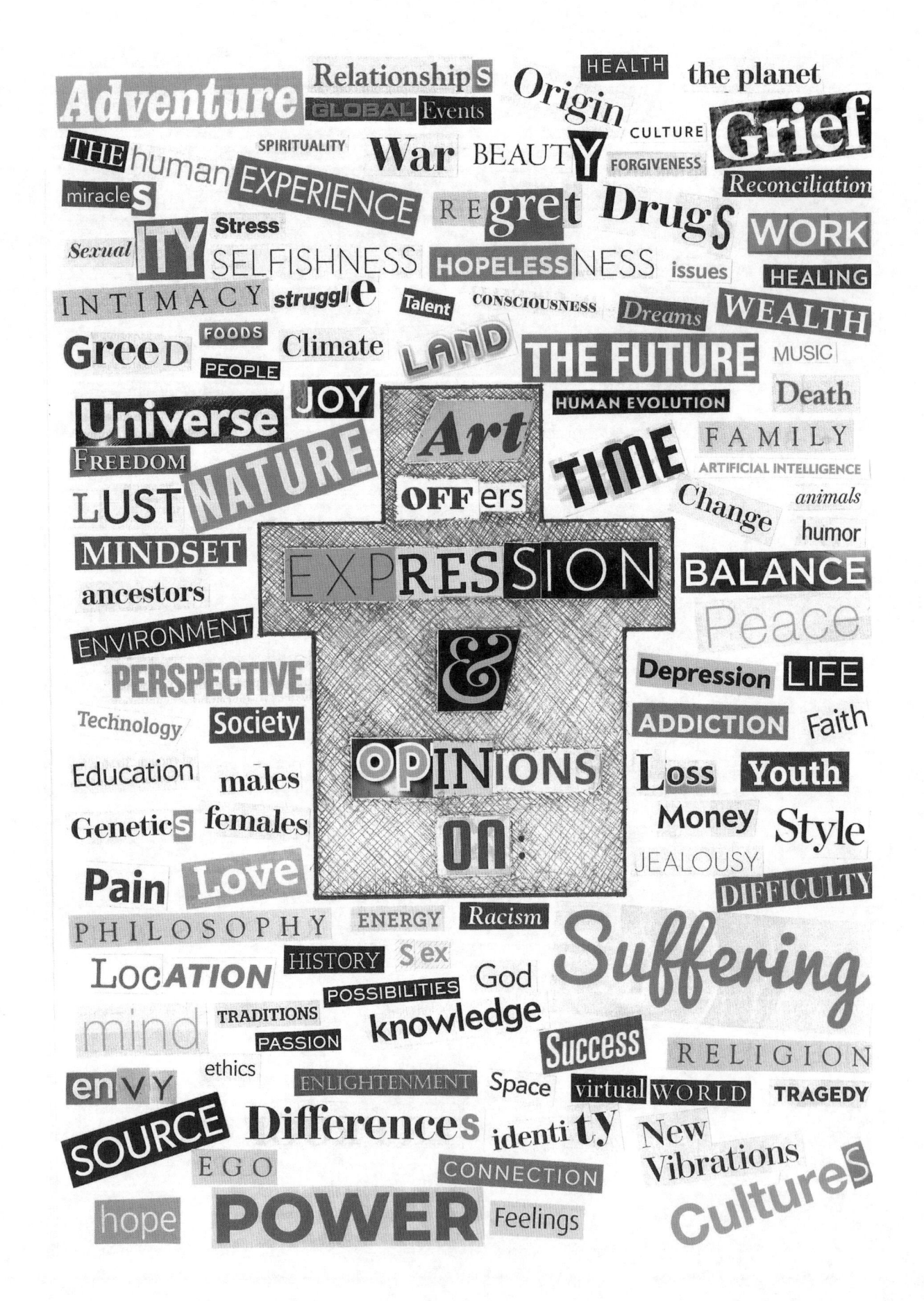

Art offers expression & opinions on: Adventure, Relationships, Health, Origin, the planet, Global Events, Culture, Grief, THE human SPIRITUALITY, War, BEAUTY, FORGIVENESS, Reconciliation, miracles, EXPERIENCE, Regret, Drugs, WORK, Sexual, ITY, Stress, HOPELESSNESS, issues, HEALING, SELFISHNESS, INTIMACY, struggle, Talent, CONSCIOUSNESS, Dreams, WEALTH, Greed, FOODS, Climate, PEOPLE, LAND, THE FUTURE, MUSIC, Universe, JOY, HUMAN EVOLUTION, Death, Freedom, NATURE, TIME, FAMILY, ARTIFICIAL INTELLIGENCE, LUST, Change, animals, humor, MINDSET, BALANCE, ancestors, Peace, ENVIRONMENT, PERSPECTIVE, Depression, LIFE, Technology, Society, ADDICTION, Faith, Education, males, Loss, Youth, Genetics, females, Money, Style, JEALOUSY, Pain, Love, DIFFICULTY, PHILOSOPHY, ENERGY, Racism, Suffering, Location, HISTORY, Sex, God, POSSIBILITIES, mind, TRADITIONS, knowledge, Success, RELIGION, PASSION, envy, ethics, ENLIGHTENMENT, Space, virtual, WORLD, TRAGEDY, SOURCE, Differences, identity, New, Vibrations, EGO, CONNECTION, Cultures, hope, POWER, Feelings

138

Sincerely embracing and appreciating works of art is a useful tool for observing and looking deeper at the world and ourselves. Art can help us express and process our emotions and feelings, ultimately encouraging us to move on and truly heal. When viewing art created by others, you do not have to love everything you see, but you can have an appreciation for the skills behind the making of it and/or the message the artist was trying to convey.

There is no need to see and understand every type of art before you begin something of your own. You do not have to be trained or even have tried a technique before you create something; it can be brand new to you.

Take a moment to contemplate what inspires you. Is there already a style of art that you are drawn to? Or is there an artist you greatly admire? Is there a type of medium or are there materials you have always wanted to try? Go with your first impulses. Write down your ideas, dreams, and desires. You might already have some ideas or concepts, like something from your childhood that you wanted to try, but never got to. Maybe it is something you saw someone else doing and you felt compelled to do it too, but couldn't or didn't at the time. Maybe there is an artist that you always admired and appreciated, and you want to make an appropriation of one of their pieces.

APPROPRIATION IN ART

What is appropriation in art? Appropriation is an artistic strategy whereby the artist deliberately copies a pre-existing work of art and alters aspects of it while maintaining a resemblance to the original. This intentional borrowing of the pre-existing work is meant as a furthering of the conversation already started by the original artist. With appropriation in art, it is usually obvious to most people where the new piece of art was inspired from, since only slight alterations are made.

If you feel inspired to appropriate a piece of art to help you express emotions, traumas, or even beauty—and do so by acknowledging the artist who inspired you—then please do it. We can learn a lot by copying things that came before us. Is that not how babies and young children learn, by copying and mimicking that which they see around them? Copying can be a strong form of flattery.

Copying art? . . .

For centuries in the Western world, artists in training at prestigious art schools built their basic skills by copying past works made by master artists.

If you feel the desire to copy a piece of artwork that you greatly admire, please do it with respect. First, acknowledge and give credit to the artist and the piece of work you reproduce. Second, I would suggest not selling it, though the piece you create will probably just be for your own healing purposes and help you through a process of release. This process could further inspire you to create something that is entirely your own and give you an opportunity to practise techniques.

◎ ◎ ◎

Another art technique or, rather, style I would like you to know more about is:
ABSTRACT ART

> **Abstract art is about:**
> - Colour
> - Form
> - Lines
> - Composition
> - Expression
>
> **Abstract art is:**
> - A visual language
> - Non-representational
> - A departure from reality

Since the techniques involved in creating an abstract piece of art are mainly colour, form, lines, and composition, and anyone can use these techniques, this style of art fits in well with the idea of *art for therapy*.

This style of art may help open up and release any concerns you may have about what to create and not having the skills to do it. Anyone can create an abstract piece of art. Research some famous abstract artworks . . . you will be surprised to see what some artists have created and called art.

Abstract art is a very open and freeing style. Instead of trying to actually represent anything, you can just focus on the materials (like the paint or clay) you are using. With the materials, the process can be just about making marks, such as:

- Planned marks
- Random marks
- Emotional marks
- Intense and fast marks
- Soft and slow marks
- Big or small marks

Remember, you are not trying to represent people, objects, places, or nature. Instead, more focus is on the technical elements of the creative process. You can have a plan for your piece—chose the colours, have ideas about the composition, etc. Or it can be an "in the moment" inspired piece, where you have no plan and just do the first things that pop into your head. This is known as creating from a *stream of consciousness*.

Abstract art can inspire emotions and reactions in the viewer in a more indirect way than representational art. Instead of a piece inspiring thought and telling a story through the representation of actual people or objects, abstract art just uses colour, lines, form, and composition to do this.

PROCESS OF EMOTIONAL RELEASE THROUGH CREATIVITY

Now that we have thought about several aspects of the creative process, take some time to do your own research about the world of art. Let yourself be guided by your emotions and the things that inspire you. Write down any ideas that come to you.

In the next chapter, I have put together ten different project ideas. You are welcome to try some of them or just use steps in the process I walk you through below for your own generated ideas.

> *Let go of the need for a "perfect" finished product when the process is complete*
> *It is more about the **process***
> *The act of creating*
> *The flow*
> *The potential release*
> *The expression*

IF USING YOUR OWN GENERATED IDEAS:

What art materials/style do you want to use?

Gather all the materials needed for the art project you intend to create.

From your research on the world of art, you may have been captivated by a certain time period or style of art. You could use this inspiration as a starting point for your own project idea and gather information on what materials are needed to create the piece.

What emotion(s) do you want to express?

Truly giving our emotions a safe space to be fully expressed will help you process and release them instead of keeping them locked up in your emotional and physical body. When we are able to authentically face and pinpoint the emotions swirling around inside of us, we may then begin the process of expressing them in helpful, safe, and productive ways.

SO, WHAT DO YOU NEED TO EXPRESS?

Grief	Jealousy	Hopelessness
Sadness	Envy	Emptiness
Anger	Regret	Forgiveness
Rage	Despair	Loneliness
Pain	Anxiety	Frustration
Dissapointment	Joy	Acceptance
Worthlessness	Love	

A GUIDE TO THE COLLECTIVE AWAKENING

FEELING IS HEALING

FOR ALL PROJECTS: SET UP A WORKING SPACE

You need a space where you will be able to execute your project. This is somewhere you can potentially make a bit of a mess and be able to possibly leave the project undisturbed for future work or to dry. You could work outside or in a garage, or if working inside, you can create a space with drop cloths, old sheets, cardboard, or old towels. I have used an old kiddy pool for messy projects, making it easy to move it around or contain runny or liquid materials.

- Working space could be inside, outside, or in a garage
- Lay down drop cloths/old towels/newspaper/cardboard
- If working on the ground, cover the area with drop cloths, etc.
    - Use a large piece of cardboard as your working surface
    - Use old pillows to sit on
- If working on a table or easel, cover the ground around it with drop cloths, etc.
    - Cover the table top, if needed
    - Have a chair or stand
- Gather all supplies needed for the project and set them up
- Put on old clothes
- Make sure there is adequate lighting
- Have drinking water and music available

⊚ ⊚ ⊚

When you have:

- Gathered all the supplies you will need
- Your working space set up
- Your project idea
- Determined which emotion(s) want to be expressed

Now:

It's time to actually start the creative process...

A GUIDE TO THE COLLECTIVE AWAKENING

THE CREATIVE PROCESS FOR EXPRESSION:

Focus on the materials selected

Focus on the emotion(s) needing to be expressed...

    How does the emotion(s) want to be expressed?

        Slowly or quickly

        Gently or firmly

        Quietly or loudly

> *Time to create*
> **No** *expectations*
> *Focused and open-minded*
> **No** *judgments*
> *This is a safe place*
> *Let your emotions guide you...*
> *Let them have control*
> *A voice*
> *Take some more deep breaths*

SET SOME INTENTIONS FOR THIS CREATIVE PROCESS:

Perhaps intentions of...

    Love

    Support

    Guidance

    Healing

    A deeper perspective

    Letting go

    Transmuting

    Understanding

    Knowledge

Viewpoint of higher self

Release

Forgiveness

CALL IN YOUR SPIRIT GUIDES—your higher self, the divine Universe, archangels, ancestors, etc.

Ask them for: help, openness, protection, guidance, support, wisdom

> *Take more deep breaths*
> *Focus on your intention(s)*
> *Focus on your spirit guide(s)*
> *Close your eyes for a moment*
> *As you focus and breathe*

Now bring your focus and awareness to what is the **cause** of the emotion(s) —what you think is the cause…

From a broader perspective—a higher dimensional perspective—many key and central aspects of this journey have already been planned out for you and by you. You are, now, just playing it out and exercising your free will with how you respond or react to the circumstances you are faced with. All your circumstances are helping you grow spiritually and awakening your consciousness to an ever-expanding divine Universe to which you are connected and a part of. Your present journey is also helping you clear out personal and ancestral karma and creating a space where you can experience, and possibly learn from, different outcomes and perspectives.

Triggers, or traumas, have been set in place to come about in times when you may be ready to shed that layer of suffering or unconsciousness. Every circumstance or person that triggers you is actually a gift wrapped in an undesirable looking package. With our limited 3D viewpoint, we have a very narrow perspective of the bigger story being played out. But this narrow perspective helps us be here fully, in this one experience, and not get distracted by the multitude of all the goings-on in the Universe.

Triggers occur. Emotions consume and possibly overwhelm you. The ego takes over and starts pointing fingers, placing blame, and judging, or it tries to understand *why* it is happening—all of this is draining your life-force energy. Remember to breathe; there is power in your breath. Try to regain the lead from the ego by focusing *only* on your breath and the emotion(s) that is arising in you. The emotion(s) that has been brought up is what is important. Even if you can prove how another person's actions are wrong or you can gain some understanding of why it happened, ultimately, *it does not matter.* You are left feeling drained, tired, and lost, and soon you will find yourself in a similar situation, being triggered all over again. The ego will continue to hold you in the perspective of victimhood, division and judgment.

> *So let all of that go and bring your entire focus to the emotion(s)*

> *When triggered...*
> ***Stop***
> *Do not **do** anything*
> *Do not **say** anything*
> *Breathe*
> *Breathe again*
> *And again... deeply*

Imagine for a moment that your ego is a little child that lives deep inside of you, and all the feelings you are being consumed and overwhelmed with are the little child's feelings. The little child is desperate for your comfort, your support, your attention, your protection, and your love. Sadly, most of the time we ignore this inner little child and instead focus our attention on the who/what/where/why/how of the outside circumstances. But what if we gave our little inner children our full attention and offered words like:

- *"How may I support you in this?"*
- *"What do you want to say? I am listening."*
- *"It is okay if you just want to be silent. I will just be here with you in silence."*
- *"I love you."*
- *"I am so sorry for your pain."*
- *"I am not going anywhere; I am here with you for as long as you need."*
- *"I will always protect you; I have your back."*
- *"You have done nothing wrong; I am not mad at you!"*
- *"I believe in you!"*

Do not *react* from the ego to:

- The person or people
- The circumstance(s)
- Beliefs
- Ideas

- The physical object(s)
- Words
- The outside world

Instead *respond* from the soul—Go inside and focus on:

- Your mind and body
- The emotion(s) you are feeling
- Where you feel that emotion in your body

Go deeper...

- What does this emotion(s) or body part want to say? Or do?
- How can you help and support this emotion(s) or body part?
- How can you hold space for your inner child?
- How can you offer comfort? A hug, some fresh air, just your attention?
- Is there a string of words or a mantra that can help express the emotion(s)?

Very important to remember...

You **do not** need to change anything or get out of the emotion(s) that has surfaced. Do not avoid, block, or push them away. Do not try to figure anything out or try to understand it. The emotion(s) that has surfaced simply wants to be fully and completely acknowledged and heard—not changed!

The emotion(s) that is surfacing requires as much time as it needs to be fully expressed. It has to be bigger than something that can be measured based on the perspective of time. Completely surrender your control to all of it. Focus on the emotion(s)... feel it and face it, entirely, with bravery, strength, and faith. Know that it will not last forever... only for as long as it needs to be present.

Expressing your emotions is a way toward the path of fully healing and transcending the cycles of karma—our own personal karma and the karma of the collective. Since everything in the divine Universe comes from the same source and is all connected, what you heal in yourself, you heal in the collective Universe! Our inner actions can have huge impacts on the outer realities we experience.

To stop this repetitive cycle (karma) we find ourselves in, we need to *respond* from the soul and not *react* from the ego. The emotions dwelling inside of you need to be authentically and fully felt. They need to be the main focus, expressed in a safe, healthy way. They cannot be rushed.

> Focus on the *emotion(s)*
> What does it feel like?
> How does it want to be expressed?
>
> *Let the emotion(s) completely consume you*
> *Let it come to the surface*
> *You are safe and protected*
> *Fe-e-e-el it!*
> *Forget the **cause** of the emotion(s)*
> *Just focus solely on the emotion(s) itself*

Pick up your materials—it is time to begin the piece

I will walk you through what I would do for **PROJECT #1 – ANGER**

(A list of supplies are on page 161)

PROJECT #1 – ANGER

- Focus on the anger inside—Let it flood to the surface

    The *anger* itself, <u>not</u> the *cause*

- Using a black felt marker, write words of anger

    Cover the canvas surface with all the words your anger wants to say

    Write them in various sizes

    Write them with the intensity of your anger

    The words can be vertical, horizontal, upside down, backwards

    Words can be layered and layered on top of each other

    No concern for spelling or legibility

    Fill the canvas until your anger has no more words

- Now prepare black acrylic paint on a pallet

On the canvas, apply the paint slowly and with intensity

Use brushes of various sizes

Cover the words previously written with the black felt marker

Make marks—slashes, long lines, and zig-zag lines

These marks can cover the whole word or only sections

- Continue to shut out any thoughts that will try to surface

    Just focus on the feeling of anger and where you feel it in your body

    Place your hands on those parts and send love

    Maybe a mantra or a string of repeated words could help hold your focus

    "I am angry! I am angry! I am angry…"

    Or use some of the personal words your anger wants to hear or say

    Do not go into the why

    Just stay with the anger itself

- Continue with the black paint, whack the brush hard on the canvas surface

    Making splotches or dabs

    Could be over the previous slashes and lines already put down

    Or on blank sections of the canvas

    Remember to lightly spray the paint being used

- Now rinse off the brushes and switch to **red** paint

    Follow some of the black lines with the red paint, be selective

    You could paint the red beside the black

    Or cover any words still visible

    Or mix and overlap, which will darken the red paint

    Let your *anger* guide where the paint goes and how it is applied

    Let the anger flow

    Let rage enter you

    Give your anger your undivided attention

    Feel it trickling out with every stroke of the brush

- Continue with the red paint, whack the brush hard on the canvas surface

    Making splotches or dabs on or around the black splotches previously applied

    Have areas with lots of marks

    Have areas that have less marks

    Leave spaces where the black is just black

    Red is just red

    And areas where their colours mix

- Check in with your anger

    Does it feel less intense?

    Maybe you feel some relief or you feel drained, tired, and need to stop

    Then walk away, leave the painting to dry

    Have a drink of water and get some fresh air

    Does it still feel intense and present?

    Continue layering the black and red paint with various marks

    Using the sharp edge of a pallet knife, scratch, scrape, and move the paint around

    Carve, cut, squish, and smear the paint

    Or grab another blank canvas and start the process over again

- If the painting is finished (or you need to be finished)...

    Step back

    Take a moment...breathe

    Thank your spirit guides for their help and support

    Acknowledge what you have just done

    Set the painting somewhere to dry

    Tidy up your working space and supplies

    Store any leftover paint in a sealable container

- When the painting is dry and considered finished

    Put it away, out of your sight—for at least a week

    Then bring it out and *look* at it again using the techniques described below

Really take some time to view and examine it

What is your reaction to the painting now?

Ponder the experience and thoughts from the creative process of this project

Remember what emotion(s) you were feeling when you created your piece

Ponder thoughts like:

- What did you feel when you created this?
- What do you feel *now* looking at it again?
- Are the feelings less intense? More intense?
- Are there other feelings surfacing?
- Does it trigger your emotions or create tension in your body?
- Do you have more to express in this piece?
- More to add or something to remove?
- Does it inspire a new project?
- Do you like the piece? Or hate it?

Possibly do some journaling or freewriting

- Decide what to do with your painting

    It could be hung on a wall

    Or it could be discarded

    It could be kept, but put away

    No need to rush the decision

    It could be used in the future as the anger unravels

LOOK AT YOUR PIECE IN DIFFERENT WAYS:

Step at least several feet back away from your project

See it from a distance

Rotate the piece (ninety degrees to the right or left, or 180 degrees)

View the piece from these different orientations

Squint your eyes or shift your eyes out of focus to blur the fine details

With a mirror:

- Turn your back to the piece and look at the reflection of it in the mirror
- By seeing the reflection, the image of the piece is reversed. This gives you a different perspective from viewing it directly.

An important part of the creative process can be just *looking*—with deep focus and awareness of all the minute details. By seeing your piece in various ways, you can gain different perspectives, see things you had not noticed before, and possibly generate new ideas for the piece in view or for future projects.

With abstract pieces, it is very common for viewers to see actual objects or faces in the image, even though the artist created a non-representational image. Our brains tend to take over when we look at things. It wants to complete the view without fully taking in the information that is there. Artists play with this often by making simple, incomplete lines and shadows to create an image your brain considers complete.

JOURNALING AND FREEWRITING OPTION:

Get a pen and small notebook or loose sheets of paper

Write down the answers to the questions above

Write down your own personal thoughts

Write a letter to someone you need to express something to

Write a list of words and phrases you really want someone to say to you

Write about your pain, concerns, or problems

A positive option for expressing emotions in a non-harmful manner

Let it just flow out of you

Just let it flow

Write the first thoughts that come to your head—*stream of consciousness*

The more you write, relax, and open up, the more the flow will *flow*

It is **not** about making sense

No need for full sentences or punctuation

Just a stream of consciousness flowing in the moment

Simply words

Can be kept, used in future art projects or destroyed

No one has to read it

This is for you only

AFTER WORKING ON A PROJECT

After working on one of the art projects I have put together, it is really important to support the mind, body, and soul. While working on these projects, a lot of emotions, feelings, thoughts, and memories may have risen to the surface. This can make anyone feel very vulnerable, and sometimes, overwhelmed. Unfortunately, this is part of the healing process, especially when we have brought up issues that were buried deep, deep down inside of us. Starting the flow, and releasing pent-up emotions, can end up flooding our whole awareness and leave us feeling worse off than before. I promise it will pass eventually and not feel so all-consuming.

Here are a few tips to support the mind, body, and soul after the creative process:

- Even if the project is not finished, stop when you need to
- Leave the space where the project was worked on
- Drink plenty of water and eat, if hungry

- Take a shower or bath with the intention of washing away unwanted energies
- Lay down and rest the body—*stillness*
- Be in nature—get some fresh air, hug a tree, or walk barefoot on the grass
- If extra support is needed, call a friend or family member
- Or call upon your higher self and spirit guides
- Listen to soothing music or music to match your mood
- Meditate or just sit still with your thoughts and emotions
- Give yourself all the time you need—examine, ponder, and work through it
- Let yourself cry, yell, scream, rant—express your emotions in a safe way
- Allow the process of integrating your healing journey

Facing our emotions, pain, and life circumstances is a step toward releasing the unwanted baggage we carry with us. This baggage affects our moods, our relationships, our state of health (physically and mentally), and the choices we make. Avoiding and burying our emotions just isn't working anymore; we have to try something new.

Giving ourselves time to really examine, experience, and ponder our emotions can create a space for integration and healing. If we can give ourselves the time to mull over the emotions inside us, it will become easier to digest all that was done, said, seen, created, felt, heard, lost, gained, exposed, and shared.

CHAPTER 11

ART PROJECTS

Chapter 11
ART PROJECTS

Below is a list of ten project ideas I have put together with the objective of expressing emotions in a creative and healthy way. For each project, there is a list of all supplies needed and a step-by-step guide to follow. However, these are just guidelines to help get you going. You can choose whether or not to follow the steps. Some of the steps might inspire you, while others may irritate or bore you. Just be open to new things, and do not let the ego stop you from trying.

One of my goals with coming up with these projects was that I wanted you to be able to create, but not have to think about what to create: not be in ego. Yes, you may be trying something brand new to you and it can be intimidating, but try to let all that go. Just focus on the steps on the pages and have no attachment to the final piece.

Please read through the entire project description before beginning the process, including the supplies and the step-by-step guide. This will help you start to generate some motivation and inspiration for the project you are about to begin.

GENERAL AND OPTIONAL SUPPLIES FOR THE CREATIVE PROCESS:

- Containers of various sizes (old plastic containers)
- Paper towel/old rags
- Rubber or latex gloves
- Old shirts and pants
- Drop cloths, old towels or sheets, large pieces of cardboard, newspaper

- Pencil and eraser

- Drawing paper

- Small writing journal

- Black felt markers (various tip sizes)

- Ruler

- Glue

- Masking tape

- Palette for paint (any sort of flat tray or lid with edges)

- Tools to paint with:

    Brushes, sponges, fork, spoon, twigs, pieces of wood, palette knives, toothbrush, cotton swab, leaves, feathers, string

- Palette knives of various sizes for mixing paint

- Spray bottle with water

- Large cardboard box or plastic bin to store all these supplies

- Easel, chair, table

- Container for leftover or extra acrylic paint:

    - Obtain a sealable lid and container, preferably long and rectangular-shaped

    - Place two to three damp paper towels in the bottom of the container

    - Place wax paper (or parchment paper) on top of damp paper towel

    - With a palette knife, scoop the extra acrylic paint onto the wax paper

    - Seal the lid completely on the container

    - If possible, store in refrigerator or cool place

    - Lightly spray with water after a few days

    - Make sure the paper towel stays damp

    - Will keep paint viable for one to two weeks

MIXING PAINT AND BRUSH CARE:

When mixing paint, always use a palette knife, **not** a paintbrush. It will wreck the brush, and paint will not be thoroughly mixed. Paint can be mixed and blended right on the surface of the canvas while painting, however. This will leave parts of the original colour intact and other parts blended.

Always start with small amounts of paint, as you can always add more, but you cannot take away once it is mixed. This is especially important with adding black; only a tiny amount is needed for a big colour change.

Remember to wash the paint off your brushes if they are not in use. Acrylic paint can dry very fast and ruin brushes. Simply swish them vigorously in the water container, then wipe them with a paper towel or rag. Swish them in water again and wipe them again until the brush is clean. Do not leave brushes in the water; this will eventually ruin them.

WHY ACRYLIC PAINT?

- Affordable and readily available in most countries
- Versatile and easy to use
- Bright and vibrant colours
- Can be:

    Watered down to be like watercolour paints

    Thickened up by adding acrylic mediums
- Very binding:

    Use like glue to stick on objects, paper, sand, etc.
- Dries quickly
- Very durable

THROUGHOUT THE CREATIVE PROCESS:

It is okay to cry, to scream, or yell

Or be completely silent

Play music to support, ignite, or comfort your emotion(s)

Remember to *breathe*

Have **no** attachment and **no** judgments about the quality of the piece

Have **no** expectations on the creative process or the final product

Check in with your body often

Move and stretch stiff body parts

Take breaks

Drink water

Have healthy snacks

If inside, go outside and get some fresh air

To keep the acrylic paint from drying out, spray it lightly and often with water

The piece never has to be completely finished

There is no time limit on how long you work on it

The piece could be worked on many times—layers upon layers of paint

You can keep the end product or throw it away

Let us get into the creative process...

A GUIDE TO THE COLLECTIVE AWAKENING

PROJECT #1

Releasing – Expressing – Holding Space for:
ANGER

Project #1 Description:

Create an abstract 2D acrylic painting, using only a black felt marker and, black and red paint. The image will be created by first writing words of anger with the black felt marker on the blank canvas. Then, apply the paint on top of the words using various marks, such as lines, splotches, dabs.

Supplies:

Black and red acrylic paint

Tools to apply paint:

    Brushes of various sizes, palette knife

Canvas or wood support—minimum of 12″ x 12″

Palette for paint

Container for water

Paper towel or rags

Spray bottle with water

Black felt marker

Step-By-Step Guide for Project #1:

Description of this project is detailed previously on pages 149 – 152

PROJECT #2

Releasing – Expressing – Holding Space for:
SADNESS

Project #2 Description:

Create a 2D acrylic painting of teardrops using various shades of blue, from dark blue to light blue. The image will be created by painting simple teardrop shapes of various sizes and layering them on top of each other. Then, using the same colours, little dots will be added to the final layer.

Supplies:

Blue, white, and black acrylic paint

Optional—red and orange acrylic paint

Tools to apply paint:

    Brushes of various sizes, palette knife

Canvas or wood support—minimum of 12″ x 12″

Palette for paint

Container for water

Paper towel or rags

Spray bottle with water

Step-By-Step Guide for Project #2:

- Focus on the *sadness* inside, let it flood to the surface

    The sadness itself, not the cause

    Read through "THE CREATIVE PROCESS FOR EXPRESSION" (pages 145-149)

    With the chosen emotion of sadness, determine:

- How to express (slow, fast, intensely, or gently)
- Spend some time pondering questions provided (page 148)
- Set intentions for the project
- Call in your higher self and spirit guides
- Set up your working space (page 144) and all supplies needed

- Prep various shades of blue—let the sadness mix the paint

  Use a palette knife to mix paint—**not a brush**

  Very dark blue—mix blue with small amount of black (6:1)

  Dark blue—mix blue with tiny amount of black (20:1)

  Blue—just the original blue you are using

  Light blue—mix blue with a small amount of white (2:1)

  Very light blue—mix small amount of blue with lots of white (1:2)

  Remember to lightly spray the acrylic paint with water

- Start with the very dark blue and dark blue paint

  On the white canvas, create outlines of various large teardrops

  Use a small pointy tip brush

  Cover most of the surface of the canvas with the teardrops

  Switch to a larger flat brush

  Fill in the teardrops completely with either very dark blue or dark blue

  Let this layer dry for a few minutes

- Continue to shut out all thoughts other than those pertaining to the emotion of sadness

  Just focus on the feelings of sadness and where you feel it in your body

  Place your hands on those parts and send *love*

  Maybe a mantra or a string of repeated words could help hold your focus

  "I am sad! I am sad! I am sad ..."

  Or use some of the personal words your sadness wants to hear or say

  Do not go to the why ... just stay with the sadness

  No need to get out of the feelings

Instead, just sit with them

It is okay to let your teardrops fall

Let the sadness pour out of you

- Rinse off brushes and switch to the original blue paint

    Create outlines of smaller teardrops directly on top of large, very dark blue teardrops

    Do this randomly, leaving some of the background teardrops untouched

    Let your teardrops be imperfect and messy

    Let this layer dry for a few minutes

    Remember to breathe

    Take a quick break—drink some water

    Lightly spray the paint with water

    If you need to, cry your heart out

    Do not hold anything back

- Rinse off brushes and switch to the light/very light blue paint

    Create outlines of even smaller teardrops directly on top of other layers

    Do this randomly and with selection

    Tears upon tears

    Upon tears and more tears

    This is the last layer, so take your time with the placement of the teardrops

    Remember to lightly spray the paint with water

- Using a small pointy brush, add dots selectively all over the canvas

    Water down the paint to make it less thick, but not runny

    With a moist brush, **not** wet, only dip the tip in the paint

    Then, create a few dots, dip in paint, create a few dots, dip in paint . . .

    Feel your sadness creating drips of despair

    Each drip is a release

    No need to rush

    An ocean can be filled

A sacred space for your sadness to just be sad

    Randomly place the dots, or create a pattern inside the teardrops

    Start with dark/very dark blue paint

    Then, blue paint

    Then, light/very light blue paint

    Could even make dots with white and black paint

    If you so desire...

    Repeat the mantra, "I am sad, I am sad, I am sad and it is okay to be sad..."

    Or your own words, while applying each dot

- Check in with your sadness

    Does it feel less intense?

    Maybe you feel some relief or you feel drained, tired, and need to stop

    Then walk away and leave the painting to dry

    Have a drink of water and get some fresh air

    Or does it still feel intense and present?

    Continue creating dots, but with red or red/orange

    Maybe apply slowly with great focus

    Or apply quickly, messily, and randomly

    Continue to give your sadness your undivided attention

    Or grab another blank canvas and start the process over again

- If the painting is finished (or you need to be finished)...

    Step back

    Take a moment—Breathe

    Thank your spirit guides for their help and support

    Acknowledge what you have just done

    Set your painting aside to dry completely

    Tidy up your working space and supplies

    Store any leftover paint in a sealable container

JENNA WALKER

Review "AFTER WORKING ON A PROJECT" (pages 154-155)

- When the painting is dry and considered finished...

    Put it away, out of your sight—for at least a week

    Then, bring it out and *look* at it again using techniques described on page 153

    Really take some time to view and examine it

    What is your reaction to the painting now?

    Ponder the experience and thoughts from the creative process of this project

    Remember what emotion(s) you were feeling when you created your piece

    Ponder thoughts like:

    What did you feel when you created this?

    What do you feel *now* looking at it again?

    Are the feelings less intense? More intense?

    Are there other feelings surfacing?

    Does it trigger your emotions or create tension in your body?

    Do you have more to express in this piece?

    More to add or something to remove?

    Does it inspire a new project?

    Do you like the piece? Or hate it?

    Possibly do some journaling or freewriting

- Decide what to do with the painting

    It could be hung on a wall

    Or it could be discarded

    It could be kept, but put away

    No need to rush the decision

    It could be used in the future as this sadness unravels

A GUIDE TO THE COLLECTIVE AWAKENING

PROJECT #3

Releasing – Expressing – Holding space for:
FORGIVENESS

Project #3 Description:

Create a 2D acrylic painting of candles lighting the path to forgiveness. Background will be gray, and then circles of various sizes will be traced out. Each circle will be painted light blue and finally, a lit candle will be painted inside.

Supplies:

White, black, light blue, yellow, orange, and red acrylic paint

Black felt marker

Circular objects for tracing (2-5 inches in diameter)

Tools to apply paint:

  Brushes of various sizes, palette knife

Canvas or wood support—minimum of 12"x 12"

Palette for paint

Container for water

Paper towel or rags

Spray bottle with water

Step-By-Step Guide for Project #3:

- Focus on someone or something you need to forgive

    You may not be ready to completely let go and forgive

    That is okay

    Just try to connect with what it might feel like to forgive

Maybe ... *relief, emptiness, a lightness, a warming sensation*

Expect a lot of resistance from the ego

Read through "THE CREATIVE PROCESS FOR EXPRESSION" (pages 145-149)

Take yourself down memory lane

Remember the person(s) or circumstances that you want to forgive

Give yourself a few minutes to feel how you were hurt

Maybe you need to forgive *yourself*

Hold an image of the person(s) or circumstance in your head

Imagine it sitting in front of you

From your heart, with as much authenticity as you can gather, say:

"I want to forgive you, I need to forgive you, I forgive you"

Or any other words of forgiveness that you feel compelled to say

With the chosen emotion of forgiveness, determine:

- How to express (slow, fast, intensely, or gently)
- Spend some time pondering questions provided (page 148)
- Set intentions for the project
- Call in your higher self and spirit guides
- Set up your working space (page 144) and all supplies needed

• Prep the canvas with an underpainting

　　On a palette, prep light gray and dark gray paint

　　Mix white and black to create two different grays

　　Completely cover the surface of the canvas with the light and dark gray

　　One side with light gray blending to the other side with the dark gray

　　Let this dry completely, clean brushes and clean up paint

　　Use this time to sit with:

　　Forgiveness

　　Your intention(s)

　　Your higher self and spirit guide(s)

Yourself (the body, mind and ego)

- With your circular objects, trace circles all over the surface of the canvas

    Use a black felt marker to trace the circular objects

    Marker can be painted over later or left to show through

    Use different sizes to create a variety of circles

    Do not overlap the circles, but they could touch

    Consider the composition and placement of the circles:

    Circles could be positioned all over, spaced evenly

    Circles could be positioned in random clusters

    Circles could be positioned with a concentration on one side

- Gather very light blue paint on your palette

    Paint the inside of each circle with the very light blue

    Use a small, flat brush for the edges

    Either paint over the black felt marker lines

    Or leave them showing through

    It does not have to be perfect

    Let the circles dry completely, clean brushes and clean up paint

    Use this time to focus on forgiveness

    Possibly repeat a mantra of forgiveness for a few minutes

    Or do some journaling or freewriting

- Inside each circle, paint a simple candle

    Prepare your palette with white, black, yellow, orange, and red paint

    You only need a small amount of each paint colour

    Remember to lightly spray your paint with water

    Start by painting a long white rectangle starting at the base of *each* circle

    This will be the main stem of the candles

    Then, at the top of each long white rectangle, paint a small black line

    This will be the wick of the candles

Now, paint the flame of each candle

With every flame you paint, light the flame of *forgiveness*

Say a mantra of forgiveness

If you cannot forgive, ask your spirit guides to do it on your behalf

Forgiveness is for you, not for the one you are forgiving

You do not need to carry this burden any longer

It is only draining your life-force energy

Let it go

For each flame, start with a yellow tear shape just above the top of the wick

Use a small pointy tip brush for painting the flames

Then, with orange, paint a smaller tear shape inside the yellow tear shape

Then, with red, paint small lines around and inside the orange tear shape

With yellow and orange paint mix with a bit of white to make them lighter

With these lighter colours, paint small lines in the centre of the flame, overlapping

- Check in with your forgiving heart

    Were you able to forgive?

    Maybe you feel some relief or you feel drained, tired, and need to stop

    Walk away and leave the painting to dry

    Have a drink of water and get some fresh air

    Were you not able to fully forgive?

    It is okay

    It may take some time, practice and patience

    Your higher self and spirit guides can help you with this

    Your higher self and spirit guides can offer forgiveness on your behalf

    By forgiving, you are **not** implying that what was done is okay

    Instead, by forgiving another person, you are releasing the pain from the experience

    You do not need to carry this burden

    It is draining your life-force energy

If desired, you could create another painting using the same steps

- If the piece is finished (or you need it to be finished) . . .

    Step back

    Take a moment—*Breathe*

    Thank your spirit guides for their help and support

    Acknowledge what you have just done

    Set your painting aside to dry completely

    Tidy up your working space and supplies

    Store any leftover paint in a sealable container

    Review "AFTER WORKING ON A PROJECT" (pages 154-155)

- When the painting is dry and considered finished . . .

    Put it away, out of your sight—for at least a week

    Then, bring it out and *look* at it again using techniques described on page 153

    Really take some time to view and examine it

    What is your reaction to the painting now?

    Ponder the experience and thoughts from the creative process of this project

    Remember what emotion(s) you were feeling when you created your piece

    Ponder thoughts like:

    What did you feel when you created this?

    What do you feel *now* looking at it again?

    Are the feelings less intense? More intense?

    Are there other feelings surfacing?

    Does it trigger your emotions or create tension in your body?

    Do you have more to express in this piece?

    More to add or something to remove?

    Does it inspire a new project?

    Do you like the piece? Or hate it?

    Possibly do some journaling or freewriting

- Decide what to do with the painting

    It could be hung on a wall

    Or it could be discarded

    It could be kept, but put away

    No need to rush the decision

    It could be used in the future as this forgiveness unravels

PROJECT #4

Cultivating – Expressing – Holding Space for:
FORGIVENESS

Project #4 Description:

Create a 2D drawing on paper of an image of someone you need to forgive. Using various pencils, a blending stick, and, if desired, colour, try your best attempt at achieving a likeness of the person from memory or use a photograph as a reference. It will only be the head and shoulders (known as a bust).

Supplies:

Drawing paper—minimum of 8" x 10"

Drawing pencils (2B, H, 2H, and 4H)

Eraser and sharpener

Blending stick

Coloured pencils

If available, a photograph of the person

Step-By-Step Guide for Project #4:

- Focus on someone you need to forgive

    You may not be ready to completely let go and forgive

    That is okay

    Just try to connect with what it might feel like to forgive

    Maybe . . . *relief, emptiness, a lightness, a warming sensation*

    Expect a lot of resistance from the ego

    Read through "THE CREATIVE PROCESS FOR EXPRESSION" (pages 145-149)

    Take yourself down memory lane

    Remember the person that you want to forgive

    Give yourself a few minutes to feel how you were hurt

    Hold an image of the person in your head or look at their photograph

    Imagine them sitting in front of you

    From your heart, with as much authenticity as you can gather, say:

    "I want to forgive you, I need to forgive you, and I forgive you"

    Or any other words of forgiveness that you feel compelled to say

    Focus solely on words of forgiveness

    Put aside judgments, reasons, questions or any hurtful words

    With the chosen emotion of forgiveness, determine:

    - How to express (slow, fast, intensely, or gently)
    - Spend some time pondering questions provided (page 148)
    - Set intentions for the project
    - Call in your higher self and spirit guides
    - Set up your working space (page 144) and all supplies needed

- Start with soft, light lines/marks to create a general outline of the head and shoulders

    Take some time to study the photograph or your memory of the person

    Focus on the shape of their head, neck, and shoulders

    This does not have to be perfect or realistic

Do the best you can and that is enough

Faces are one of the hardest things to draw

This is just for you

It is okay if it looks like a child's drawing

Let your inner child draw

With a 4H pencil, lightly sketch out the shape of the head, neck, and shoulders

By sketching lightly, erasing unwanted lines or marks will be easier

Continue until you are content with the outline

- With soft, light lines/marks, create a general outline of the eyes, nose, and mouth

    Using the photograph, or your memory

    Focus on the shape of their eyes, nose, and mouth

    With a 4H pencil, lightly sketch their eyes, nose, and mouth

    Determine how close together their eyes are

    Then, look at where their nose is in relation to the eyes

    Determine the shape of their nose

    Then, look at where their mouth is in relation to the nose

    Determine the shape of their mouth

    Keep looking back to the photograph or your memory

    Study each part slowly and with focus

- With soft, light lines/marks, create a general outline of the hair and ears

    Again, using the photograph, or your memory

    Focus on the length and texture of their hair

    If their hair is short, focus on the shape of their ears

    Still using a 4H pencil, lightly sketch their hair and ears

    Determine where their hair is parted—in the middle, or to one side

    Is their hair straight, wavy, or curly?

    Is it long, short, or medium length?

    After lightly sketching out their hair, determine where their ears are

- See the simple shapes that make their ears
- Compare where the ears are with relation to their eyes and nose
- Now that a general, light outline of the person is complete, darken the lines
  - Using an H or 2B pencil, slowly trace over the lines already drawn
  - Start with the contour lines of their face, neck, and shoulders
  - The 2B pencil will be much darker and harder to erase than the 4H pencil
  - So, slowly build up the lines you have already laid down
  - Erase any lighter lines from the first layer drawn with a 4H pencil
  - Darken the eyes and mouth with the 2B pencil
  - For the nose, use only light marks with the 2B pencil for the nostrils
  - For the bridge of the nose, use a blending stick to rub light lines
  - Create a shadow at the bridge of the nose and under the eyes to create form
  - Darken the hair and ears, if visible
  - Hair can be created with lines upon lines, a slow build up and layering of lines
  - Then, using the blending stick, hair lines can be softened and blended
  - Ears only need to be simple lines and shapes
  - Use the blending stick to create form and shadows in the ears
- Final touches to eyes, mouth, hair, and shoulders
  - Using an H pencil, add more tiny details to the eyes
  - Focus on the iris, the corner of the eyes, and the soft lines around the eyes
  - Build up the eyelashes with soft, curved lines
  - Add little details to the lips with small lines following the inside
  - Add more light lines to the hair
  - At the base of the neck, create a simple collar of their shirt
  - Collar can be round, square, or v-shaped
  - Tidy up any unwanted lines with eraser
- If desired, colour may be added to your drawing
  - Start by lightly adding colour and slowly build it up

Colour the skin of the face and neck

Add colour to their eyes and lips

Add colour to their hair, blending in with your pencil marks

Finally, add colour to their shirt

Or just leave the drawing colourless

- If the drawing is finished (or you need to be finished) . . .

    Step back

    Take a moment—Breathe

    Have a drink of water and get some fresh air

    Find somewhere quiet and comfortable to sit with your drawing

    Take some time to look at the drawing, at the face staring back at you

    Feel whatever you are feeling

    No need to get out of the feeling

    Let it come to the surface

    Put aside judgments, reasons, questions, or any hurtful words

    Let go of the story behind the pain

    It is time to put down this burden you carry

    The pain, the anger, the sadness

    It is time for forgiveness

    Look into the face of the one you drew

    From your heart, with as much authenticity as you can gather, say:

    "I want to forgive you, I need to forgive you, and I forgive you"

    Or *"I forgive you for what you did,*

    You were not acting from a place of love,

    You were acting from your own place of pain,

    I send you light and love,

    May you find healing and resolution,

    So no future victims will be harmed by your unprocessed pain, and so it is."

A GUIDE TO THE COLLECTIVE AWAKENING

Or any other words of forgiveness that you feel compelled to say

Focus solely on words of forgiveness

If you just cannot forgive at this time... *it is okay*

Ask your higher self and spirit guides to forgive on your behalf

Regain your life-force energy by forgiving

Thank your spirit guides for their help and support

Acknowledge what you have just done

Tidy up your working space and supplies

Review "AFTER WORKING ON A PROJECT" (pages 154-155)

- Continuing the process of forgiveness...

    Put your drawing away, out of your sight—for at least a week

    Then, bring it out and *look* at it again using techniques described on page 153

    Really take some time to view and examine it

    What is your reaction to the drawing now?

    Ponder the experience and thoughts from the creative process of this project

    Remember what emotion(s) you were feeling when you created your drawing

    Ponder thoughts like:

    What did you feel when you created this?

    What do you feel *now* looking at it again?

    Are the feelings less intense? More intense?

    Are there other feelings surfacing?

    Does it trigger your emotions or create tension in your body?

    Do you have more to express in this piece?

    More to add or something to remove?

    Does it inspire a new project?

    Do you like the piece? Or hate it?

    Possibly do some journaling or freewriting

- Decide what to do with the drawing

It could be hung on a wall

Or it could be discarded

It could be kept, but put away

No need to rush the decision

It could be used in the future as this forgiveness unravels

◎ ◎ ◎

PROJECT #5

Releasing – Expressing – Holding Space for:
DESPAIR AND HOPELESSNESS

Project #5 Description:

Create a simple 2D drawing of spirals. With white drawing paper, and black and yellow felt markers, the image will be created by making spirals of various sizes. In a fast-paced, automatic way, create numerous spirals through repetition. See 'APPENDIX' – Fig. 1 on page 215 for a visual guide.

Supplies:

Black and yellow felt marker

Drawing paper—minimum of 8" x 10"

Table top or drawing board

Step-By-Step Guide for Project #5:

- Focus on the feelings of *despair* and *hopelessness* from deep within you

    Let the feelings flood to the surface—Just the feelings, not the cause

Read through "THE CREATIVE PROCESS FOR EXPRESSION" (pages 145-149)

With the chosen emotion of despair and hopelessness, determine:

- How to express (slow, fast, intensely, or gently)
- Spend some time pondering questions provided (page 148)
- Set intentions for the project
- Call in your higher self and spirit guides
- Set up your working space (page 144) and all supplies needed

- With drawing paper and black felt marker, begin drawing spirals

    Focus your attention of the despair and hopelessness you feel

    Take several deep breaths

    Come into an open, meditative state

    You are going to just draw and not think about what you are doing

    No planning, concern for composition, or placement of marks

    Automatic drawing

    Start making spirals with the black felt marker anywhere on the paper

    From the middle point, circle around and around, slowly increasing the size

    Circle around at least three to five times to create your spirals

    It is okay if the lines overlap or are not spaced perfectly

    Draw them in different sizes and randomly all over the paper

    Your spirals can overlap each other

    Draw the despair and hopelessness circling within you

    Feel it being comforted, acknowledged, and recognized

    No need to get out of the feelings

    Instead, just sit with them

    Draw until the page is full of spirals

- Continue to shut out any thoughts on the cause of the emotion that may surface

    Just focus on the actual feelings of despair and hopelessness

    Where do you feel it in your body?

Place your hands on those parts and send *love*

Maybe a mantra or a string of repeated words could help hold your focus

"It is okay that it is not okay"

Or *"I am here with you"*

Or some of the words your despair and hopelessness wants to hear

- Now, with the yellow felt marker, continue to draw spirals

    You could draw yellow spirals randomly all over the paper

    Or with the yellow, you could follow the black spirals already drawn

    Continue with the automatic drawing technique

    Just draw without thinking or planning

    Continue to let the despair and hopelessness pour out of you

    Fill the paper with yellow spirals

    Yellow spirals of sacred healing light

    Sacred light circling around your despair and hopelessness

    Let it flow, let it be

    It is okay to feel this way

    For as long as you feel this way

    Continue to add as many yellow spirals to the drawing as you desire

    Layers and layers of spirals overlapping

- Check in with your despair and hopelessness

    Does it feel less intense?

    Maybe you feel some relief or you feel drained, tired, and need to stop

    Walk away, have a drink of water, and get some fresh air

    Does it still feel intense and present?

    Continue creating more black and yellow spirals on the paper

    Or with just your finger, trace around the spirals

    Repeat the mantra from previous step . . . *"It is okay that it is not okay"*

    Or *"I am here with you"*

Or some of the words your despair and hopelessness wants to hear

Continue to give your despair and hopelessness your undivided attention

Or grab another blank piece of drawing paper and start the process over again

- If the drawing is finished (or you need to be finished) . . .

    Step back

    Take a moment—Breathe

    Look at your creation of despair and hopelessness

    Acknowledge what you have just done

    Thank your spirit guides for their help and support

    Tidy up your working space and supplies

    Review "AFTER WORKING ON A PROJECT" (pages 154-155)

- Continuing the healing process . . .

    Put your drawing away, out of your sight—for at least a week

    Then, bring it out and *look* at it again using techniques described on page 153

    Really take some time to view and examine it

    What is your reaction to the drawing now?

    Ponder the experience and thoughts from the creative process of this project

    Remember what emotion(s) you were feeling when you created your drawing

    Ponder thoughts like:

    What did you feel when you created this?

    What do you feel *now* looking at it again?

    Are the feelings less intense? More intense?

    Are there other feelings surfacing?

    Does it trigger your emotions or create tension in your body?

    Do you have more to express in this piece?

    More to add or something to remove?

    Does it inspire a new project?

    Do you like the piece? Or hate it?

Possibly do some journaling or freewriting

- Decide what to do with the drawing

    It could be hung on a wall

    Or it could be discarded

    It could be kept, but put away

    No need to rush the decision

    It could be used in the future as the despair and hopelessness unravels

PROJECT #6

Releasing – Expressing – Holding Space for:
JEALOUSY

Project #6 Description:

Create a simple 2D drawing of lines in groups of three. With white drawing paper and, black and green felt markers, the image will be created by making lines in groups of three of various sizes and lengths, in an automatic drawing technique and through repetition. See 'APPENDIX' – Fig. 2 on page 215 for a visual guide.

Supplies:

Black and green felt marker

Drawing paper—minimum of 8" x 10"

Table top or drawing board

Step-By-Step Guide for Project #6:

- Focus on the feelings of *jealousy* from deep within you

    Let the feelings of jealousy flood to the surface

    Just the feelings, not the cause

    Read through "THE CREATIVE PROCESS FOR EXPRESSION" (pages 145-149)

    With the chosen emotion of jealousy, determine:

    - How to express (slow, fast, intensely, or gently)
    - Spend some time pondering questions provided (page 148)
    - Set intentions for the project
    - Call in your higher self and spirit guides
    - Set up your working space (page 144) and all supplies needed

- With drawing paper and black felt marker, begin drawing lines in groups of three

    Focus your attention on the jealousy you feel

    Take several deep breaths

    Come into an open, meditative state

    You are going to just draw and not think about what you are doing

    Only focus on your jealousy and creating three parallel lines at a time

    No planning, concern for composition, or placement of marks

    Automatic drawing

    Draw parallel lines in groups of three, with black felt marker, anywhere on the paper

    Make the three parallel lines in the group the same length and size

    Draw some of the group of three lines horizontally and others vertically

    Draw them in different sizes and randomly all over the paper

    Jump around the paper, haphazardly creating the parallel lines in groups of three

    Do not overlap the lines

    Fill in at least half of the drawing paper with the black felt marker

- Continue to shut out any thoughts of the *cause* of the jealousy that will try to surface

    Just focus on the actual feelings of jealousy

Where do you feel it in your body?

Place your hands on those parts and send *love*

Maybe a mantra or a string of repeated words could help hold your focus

"I am jealous! I am so jealous! I am jealous!"

Or *"I am jealous, but that is okay"*

Or some of the words your jealousy wants to hear or say

- Now, using a green felt marker, continue to draw parallel lines in groups of three

    With green, fill in the empty spaces on the drawing paper

    Make the three parallel lines in the group the same length and size

    Continue with the automatic drawing technique

    And continue to let the jealousy pour out of you

    Carry on randomly jumping around the paper

    Or start at one side of the paper and work across

    Draw some of the green groups of three lines horizontally and others vertically

    Draw some of the groups larger and others, small

    Let the green represent your jealousy

    Let it flow, let it be

    It is okay to feel this way

    Why? . . . Because you are feeling this way

    Continue to add green parallel lines in groups of three to fill the drawing paper

- Check in with your jealousy

    Does it feel less intense?

    Maybe you feel some relief or you feel drained, tired, and need to stop

    Then walk away, have a drink of water, and get some fresh air

    Does it still feel intense and present?

    Continue creating more green parallel lines in groups of three

    Tiny groups of lines, until the paper is completely full

    Repeat the mantras from previous step . . .

"I am jealous! I am so jealous! I am jealous!"

Or *"I am jealous, but that is okay"*

Or some of the words your jealousy wants to hear or say

Continue to give your jealousy your undivided attention

Or grab another blank piece of drawing paper and start the process over again

- If the drawing is finished (or you need to be finished)...

    Step back

    Take a moment—Breathe

    Look at your creation of jealousy

    Acknowledge what you have just done

    Thank your spirit guides for their help and support

    Tidy up your working space and supplies

    Review "AFTER WORKING ON A PROJECT" (pages 154-155)

- Continuing the process of acknowledging your *jealousy*...

    Put your drawing away, out of your sight—for at least a week

    Then, bring it out and *look* at it again using techniques described on page 153

    Really take some time to view and examine it

    What is your reaction to the drawing now?

    Ponder the experience and thoughts from the creative process of this project

    Remember what emotion(s) you were feeling when you created your drawing

    Ponder thoughts like:

    What did you feel when you created this?

    What do you feel *now* looking at it again?

    Are the feelings less intense? More intense?

    Are there other feelings surfacing?

    Does it trigger your emotions or create tension in your body?

    Do you have more to express in this piece?

    More to add or something to remove?

Does it inspire a new project?

Do you like the piece? Or hate it?

Possibly do some journaling or freewriting

- Decide what to do with the drawing

    It could be hung on a wall

    Or it could be discarded

    It could be kept, but put away

    No need to rush the decision

    It could be used in the future as your jealousy unravels

PROJECT #7

Cultivating – Expressing – Holding Space for:
SELF-REFLECTION AND SELF ACCEPTANCE

Project #7 Description:

Create a 2D acrylic painting of reflection. Using black, white, and three colours of your choice, the image will be created on one side and then a reflection of that image will be created on the other side. Applying the chosen three colours will be done using carrots for a stamping technique. See 'APPENDIX' – Fig. 3 on page 215 for a visual guide.

> **Supplies:**
>
> Three colours of your choice, white and black acrylic paint
>
> Tools to apply paint:
>
> > Three carrots of different sizes, small pointy tip brush, large flat brush
>
> Sharp knife (to cut off the tips of the carrots)
>
> Canvas or wood support—minimum of 12" x 12"
>
> H or 2B Pencil, masking tape, ruler
>
> Palette for paint
>
> Container for water
>
> Paper towel or rags
>
> Spray bottle with water

Step-By-Step Guide for Project #7:

- Focus on the idea of self-reflection and self-acceptance

    Take some time to reflect on who you are and how to accept *all* of it

    Read through "THE CREATIVE PROCESS FOR EXPRESSION" (pages 145-149)

    With self-reflection and self-acceptance in mind, determine:

    - How to express (slow, fast, intensely, or gently)
    - Spend some time pondering questions provided (page 148)
    - Set intentions for the project
    - Call in your higher self and spirit guides
    - Set up your working space (page 144) and all supplies needed

- Prep the canvas with underpainting

    Half of the canvas will be painted black

    The other half will remain white

Determine the centre line of the canvas with a ruler

Draw the centre line with a pencil and ruler

With masking tape, place the tape along the centre line

Make sure to press down and secure the tape to the surface

With black paint and large flat brush, cover half the canvas completely

May need two coats to cover all white areas

Let the black paint dry completely

Take some time to reflect on your attributes, traits, and qualities

Reflect on the positive and the negative

Write a list, journal, or do some freewriting

What makes you, you?

When dry, slowly remove the masking tape

- With an H or 2B pencil, draw reflecting triangles

    Start with the black side of the canvas facing up

    Using a ruler, draw three triangles of different heights and sizes

    Draw the two outside triangles first, then fit in the middle triangle

    Now, rotate the canvas so the white side is facing up

    As best as you can, draw a reflection of the identical triangles from the black side

    Use the ruler to determine measurements and placement

    From the centre line, the triangles will meet and create a diamond shape

- Trace over the pencil lines with paint

    Prepare a small amount of black and white paint on your palette

    Use a small brush with a pointy tip

    On the black side of the canvas, use white paint to trace over pencil lines

    On the white side of the canvas, use black paint to trace over pencil lines

    Lines do not have to be perfect

    Let them be what they will be

    Accept the best lines you can create by hand

If needed...

    Use the black paint to fix up white lines

    Use the white paint to fix up the black lines

    But wait until the original painted lines are dry to do this

    Remember to lightly spray the acrylic paint with water

- Prep carrots and coloured paint

    Gather three carrots of different widths

    With a knife, chop off the tips of the three carrots

    Make sure it is a clean cut, leaving a flat surface

    Choose up to three colours to use in your painting

    Or use three shades of the same colour (ex. Light blue, blue and dark blue)

    Prepare the three colours on your palette

    Lightly spray the acrylic paint with water

- Take a few moments to focus on the previous reflections you pondered

    What makes you, you?

    Go deeper than your roles, labels, or job descriptions

    Take some deep breaths

    Bring out the list of your attributes, traits, and qualities

    Look at all the good ones and all the bad ones

    Honour the good ones

    Accept the bad ones

    Take a moment to really feel a sense of honour of who you are

    Feel acceptance for anything you think is lacking or bad

    Maybe a mantra or a string of repeated words could help

    "*I honour my strengths and accept my weaknesses*"

    Or "*I am sacred, I am divine, I am enough*"

    Or create your own mantras using words from your list of attributes, traits and qualities

- Use a stamping technique to create your image of reflection

Start with the biggest carrot

Dip the flat end of the carrot you cut in the 1st colour of paint

Make sure to just dip the tip of the carrot

Then stamp the flat end with paint *inside* the triangles on the canvas

Stamp a few times before re-dipping in paint

Creating lighter impressions as the paint is used up

Whatever you stamp on the black side, stamp the same on the white side

Try to create a mirror image of the black and white side

Focus your attention on self-reflection and self-acceptance

With each stamp, say aloud your attributes, traits, and qualities

The good ones and the bad ones

Reflection and acceptance

Rinse carrot tip in water and wipe off with paper towel/rags

Repeat these steps with the 2nd and 3rd colours, still using the biggest carrot

It is okay if the colours mix or stamp impressions overlap

Just remember to do the same stamps on the opposite side

Then repeat these steps with the other two carrots

Remember to lightly spray paint with water

- Check in with the feelings brought up by self-reflection and self-acceptance

    Have you deeply reflected on who you are?

    Have you genuinely accepted all that makes *you*, you?

    Maybe you feel content, relaxed, and even happy

    Or maybe you feel overwhelmed, drained, or tired and need to stop

    Then walk away and leave the painting to dry

    Have a drink of water and get some fresh air

    Or you could continue adding to the painting

    Using the small brush with a pointy tip, add small dots to the painting

    Create various dots *outside* the triangles

Use black, white, and your chosen three colours

            Remember to create a reflection

            Whatever you do on the black side, do the same on the white side

- If the painting is finished (or you need to be finished)...

            Step back

            Take a moment—Breathe

            Thank your spirit guides for their help and support

            Acknowledge what you have just done

            Set your painting aside to dry completely

            Tidy up your working space and supplies

            Store any leftover paint in a sealable container

            Review "AFTER WORKING ON A PROJECT" (pages 154-155)

- When the painting is dry and considered finished...

            Put it away, out of your sight—for at least a week

            Then, bring it out and *look* at it again using techniques described on page 153

            Really take some time to view and examine it

            What is your reaction to the painting now?

            Ponder the experience and thoughts from the creative process of this project

            Remember what emotion(s) you were feeling when you created your painting

            Ponder thoughts like:

            What did you feel when you created this?

            What do you feel *now*, when looking at it again?

            Are the feelings less intense? More intense?

            Are there other feelings surfacing?

            Does it trigger your emotions or create tension in your body?

            Do you have more to express in this piece?

            More to add or something to remove?

            Does it inspire a new project?

Do you like the piece? Or hate it?

Possibly do some journaling or freewriting

- Decide what to do with the painting

    It could be hung on a wall

    Or it could be given away as a gift

    It could be kept, but put away

    Or it could be discarded

    No need to rush the decision

    It could be used in the future as your self-acceptance and love grows

PROJECT #8

Cultivating Expressing Holding Space for:
SELF-LOVE AND HEALING

Project #8 Description:

Create a 2D mixed-media piece of self-love. The image will be created, first, by prepping the canvas with an underpainting of a giant heart, and then pasting on words cut out from magazines, newspapers, flyers or make your own. Self-love is extremely important on this healing journey. In order to love others and the world around us, we must first truly love ourselves and remember our sacredness, uniqueness, and worth.

> **Supplies:**
>
> Yellow, green and white acrylic paint
>
> Tools for painting:
>
> > Sponge, brushes of various sizes and palette knife
>
> Canvas or wood support—minimum of 12" x 12"
>
> Palette for paint
>
> Container for water
>
> Paper towels or rags
>
> Spray bottle with water
>
> Modge Podge™ or acrylic medium (glossy or matte)
>
> Magazines, newspapers, flyers, old cards, etc.
>
> Scissors
>
> Piece of flat cardboard and scrap paper

Step-By-Step Guide for Project #8:

- Focus on the feelings of *love*, let the love flood to the surface

    Contemplate some of the things you love about yourself

    Things you do/have done, your attributes, your traits—write a list

    Read through "THE CREATIVE PROCESS FOR EXPRESSION" (pages 145-149)

    With self-love and healing in mind, determine:

    - How to express (slow, fast, intensely, or gently)
    - Spend some time pondering questions provided (page 148)
    - Set intentions for the project
    - Call in your higher self and spirit guides
    - Set up your working space (page 144) and all supplies needed

- Prep the canvas with underpainting

Prepare your palette with yellow and green paint

Cut the sponge into small, rectangular pieces

Using the small piece of sponge, lightly dip a flat edge into yellow paint

Dab the sponge on scrap paper, to remove excessive paint

You want a thin layer of paint, to create impressions of the sponge texture

Now lightly dab the sponge on the canvas creating a layer of yellow

Focus on the feelings of self-love

Focus on the healing energies of the divine Universe

Then using a new piece of sponge, repeat previous steps with green paint

Slowly build up layers

Maybe leave areas just yellow or just green

Have areas where the paint overlaps and colours mix

- Paint a large white heart

    The underpainting may or may not be dry

    Either way, proceed with painting a large white heart

    If yellow and green sponge impressions are still wet, let the colours and the white mix

    Prep some white paint on your palette

    Use a medium, flat brush

    Paint the large heart in the centre of the canvas

    Imagine you are painting your heart

    Feel your heart-space

    Feel it open and pulse with fresh new energy

    Take some deep breaths

    Feel your heart beating new life-force energy throughout your body

    Maybe a mantra or a string of repeated words could help harness feelings of self-love

    "I am love, I am loving, and I am loved"

    Or create your own mantra using words from your list of attributes and achievements

    Set the canvas aside to dry completely

- Prep clippings of words from magazines, newspapers, flyers, old cards, etc.

    Find words to express and represent your strengths, achievements, attributes, and traits

    Find words of love and support that you wish to hear

    Find words that symbolize *love* and *healing*

    Make your own words with cut-out letters or write your own

    Cut them out with care and set them aside

    Gather as many as you can, though you may not use them all

- Attach and paste clippings of words onto canvas

    Prep some Modge Podge™ or acrylic medium on your palette

    These materials will work like glue to adhere the clippings to the canvas

    Gather your clippings, a piece of flat cardboard, and a medium flat brush

    Use the flat piece of cardboard as your working surface

    Place a cut-out word on the cardboard, with the word facing down

    On the backside of the cut-out, apply a thin layer of Modge Podge™

    Then apply a thin layer on the canvas where the word will be placed

    Immediately place the wet cut-out word on the canvas

    Once in position, apply another thin layer of Modge Podge™ on top of the cut-out

    Randomly place the cut-out words all over the canvas

    Place them vertically, horizontally, upside down

    Place them inside and outside the white heart you painted

    Fill and surround the heart with words of love and healing

    As you place each cut-out word, repeatedly say the word out loud

- Check in with the feelings brought up by focusing on self-love and healing

    Maybe you feel dissatisfied, frustrated, or tired and need to stop

    Then walk away and leave the painting to dry

    Have a drink of water and get some fresh air

    Come back to the painting later, when you have had time to refresh

    Try again to cultivate feelings of self-love

Self-love will grow if given time and focus

Were you able to feel strong sensations of love for yourself?

Have you genuinely appreciated all that makes you, you?

Maybe you feel content, relaxed, and even happy

You could continue adding to the painting

Using a small brush with a pointy tip, add small dots to the painting

Use the yellow and green paint

You could place dots around the cut-out words and the heart

Or you could place dots randomly all over the surface of the canvas

- If the painting is finished (or you need to be finished)...

    Step back

    Take a moment—Breathe

    Thank your spirit guides for their help and support

    Acknowledge what you have just done

    Set your painting aside to dry completely

    Tidy up your working space and supplies

    Store any leftover paint in a sealable container

    Review "AFTER WORKING ON A PROJECT" (pages 154-155)

- When the painting is dry and considered finished...

    Put it away, out of your sight—for at least a week

    Then, bring it out and *look* at it again using techniques described on page 153

    Really take some time to view and examine it

    What is your reaction to the painting now?

    Ponder the experience and thoughts from the creative process of this project

    Remember what emotion(s) you were feeling when you created your painting

    Ponder thoughts like:

    What did you feel when you created this?

    What do you feel *now* looking at it again?

Are the feelings less intense? More intense?

Are there other feelings surfacing?

Does it trigger your emotions or create tension in your body?

Do you have more to express in this piece?

More to add or something to remove?

Does it inspire a new project?

Do you like the piece? Or hate it?

Possibly do some journaling or freewriting

- Decide what to do with the painting

    It could be hung on a wall

    Or it could be given away as a gift

    It could be kept, but put away

    Or it could be discarded

    No need to rush the decision

    It could be used in the future as your self-love grows

PROJECT # 9

Cultivating – Expressing – Holding Space for:
OPEN HEART-SPACE AND LOVE OF NATURE

Project #9 Description:

Create a 2D painting by creating a grid of squares and filling in each square with shapes and symbols inspired by nature. Use three colours of your choice, black and white acrylic paint. See 'APPENDIX' – Fig. 4 for examples of shapes and symbols inspired by nature and Fig. 5 for a grid example on page 215.

> **Supplies:**
>
> Three colours of your choice, black and white acrylic paint
>
> Tools for painting:
>
> > Brushes of various sizes and palette knife
>
> Canvas or wood support—minimum of 12″ x 12″
>
> Palette for paint
>
> Container for water
>
> Paper towels or rags
>
> Spray bottle with water
>
> Pencil
>
> Black felt marker with a thick tip
>
> Ruler
>
> Scrap paper

Step-By-Step Guide for Project #9:

- Focus on opening your heart-space to the magnificent beauty of nature

    Contemplate some of the things you love about nature

    The sky, trees, plants, animals, insects, mountains, bodies of water, etc.

    Write a detailed list of things in nature that you love and appreciate

    Read through "THE CREATIVE PROCESS FOR EXPRESSION" (pages 145-149)

    With an open heart-space and love of nature in mind, determine:

    - How to express (slow, fast, intensely, or gently)
    - Spend some time pondering questions provided (page 148)
    - Set intentions for the project
    - Call in your higher self and spirit guides
    - Set up your working space (page 144) and all supplies needed

- Create a grid of squares covering the entire surface of the canvas

    First determine how big the squares will be

    Squares should be at least 1" x 1"

    If canvas is 12" x 12", then draw eleven lines horizontally and eleven lines vertically

    Each line is spaced by one inch

    Draw lines with a pencil and ruler first

    Then, use ruler and black felt marker with thick tip to trace over pencil lines

    It does **not** have to be perfect

    See 'APPENDIX' – Fig. 5 on page 215

- Generate ideas to fill in squares with shapes and symbols that represent nature

    Take a moment to breathe

    Focus on your heart-space

    Close your eyes and fill your thoughts with the natural world that surrounds you

    Possibly spend some actual time outside in nature

    Reflect on your detailed list of things in nature that you love and appreciate

    Remember, you are a part of this beautiful divine creation

    You are completely connected

    Consider some shapes and symbols that represent nature

    Such as: *waves, water drops, leaves, trees, flowers, blades of grass, insects, birds*

    Or: *circles, swirls, lines, dots, stars, triangles, puffy clouds*

    See 'APPENDIX' – Fig. 4 on page 215 for examples

    With a pencil and paper, practise drawing some shapes and symbols

    Remember to keep them simple

    You are not going to paint, let's say, an actual detailed bird

    Instead use simple lines, shapes and marks that represent a bird

- Prepare three colours, black and white acrylic paint

    Choose three colours that represent the parts of nature you wish to express

    Each chosen colour can be lightened with white or darkened with black

On your palette, place a small amount of each colour, black and white

Use small pointy tip brushes

Remember to lightly spray paint with water as you work

- Fill in the squares with an open heart-space and a love of nature

    You may want to follow a theme for the entire painting

    Such as a theme of trees or flowers or water or insects

    Or you may want each square to represent something different from nature

    Focus solely on one square at a time

    With a medium angled flat brush, you could first fill in the square a solid colour

    Let it dry completely

    Then add your chosen shapes and symbols on top

    Or paint your shapes and symbols with the white of the canvas as your background

    As you paint each square, focus on the magnificent beauty of nature

    Maybe a mantra or a string of repeated words could help hold your focus

    "Nature is beautiful, nature provides, nature is life"

    Or create a mantra from your list of things in nature that you love and appreciate

    Feel love for the tiny details

    Feel love for the simplicity, strength, and abundance of the natural world

    Feel your connection to nature

    Feel the nature inside of you

    Continue until all squares are filled in

    This project may take more than one sitting

- Check in with the feelings brought up from focusing on your heart-space and nature

    Maybe you feel dissatisfied, frustrated, or tired and need to stop

    Then walk away and leave the painting to dry

    Have a drink of water and get some fresh air

    Come back to the painting later, when you have had time to refresh

    Try again to cultivate an open heart-space and feelings of love for nature

A GUIDE TO THE COLLECTIVE AWAKENING

Love will grow if given time and focus

Were you able to maintain an open heart-space and feelings of love for nature?

Have you genuinely appreciated the magnificent beauty of the natural world?

Maybe you feel deeply connected, alive, happy, and thankful

You could continue adding to the painting

Using a small pointy tip brush, add in tiny dots in a selection of squares

Imagine they are tiny dots of divine life-force energy

- If the painting is finished (or you need to be finished) . . .

    Step back

    Take a moment—Breathe

    Thank your spirit guides for their help and support

    Acknowledge what you have just done

    Set your painting aside to dry completely

    Tidy up your working space and supplies

    Store any leftover paint in a sealable container

    Review "AFTER WORKING ON A PROJECT" (pages 154-155)

- When the painting is dry and considered finished . . .

    Put it away, out of your sight—for at least a week

    Then, bring it out and *look* at it again using techniques described on page 153

    Really take some time to view and examine it

    What is your reaction to the painting now?

    Ponder the experience and thoughts from the creative process of this project

    Remember what emotion(s) you were feeling when you created your painting

    Ponder thoughts like:

    What did you feel when you created this?

    What do you feel *now* looking at it again?

    Are the feelings less intense? More intense?

    Are there other feelings surfacing?

Does it trigger your emotions or create tension in your body?

Do you have more to express in this piece?

More to add or something to remove?

Does it inspire a new project?

Do you like the piece? Or hate it?

Possibly do some journaling or freewriting

- Decide what to do with the painting

    It could be hung on a wall

    Or it could be given away as a gift

    It could be kept, but put away

    Or it could be discarded

    No need to rush the decision

    It could be used in the future as your love of nature grows

PROJECT #10

Cultivating – Expressing – Holding Space for:
LOVE

Project #10 Description:

Create a 2D acrylic painting to enhance and cultivate the feelings of love. The image will be created by first drawing a simple outline of a rainbow filling the entire canvas surface. Then, each section of the rainbow outline will be filled in with little coloured hearts. See 'APPENDIX' – Fig. 6 for examples of rainbow outlines on page 215.

> **Supplies:**
>
> Red, orange, yellow, green, dark blue, dark purple, white acrylic paint
>
> Tools for painting:
>
> > Small brush with pointy tip and small angled brush
>
> Canvas or wood support—minimum of 12" x 12"
>
> Palette for paint
>
> Container for water
>
> Paper towels or rags
>
> Spray bottle with water
>
> Scrap paper
>
> Thick black felt marker
>
> H Pencil
>
> Ruler

Step-By-Step Guide for Project #10:

- Focus on opening your heart-space to the feelings of love

    Contemplate some things you love—*about yourself, others, places, things, etc.*

    Write a detailed list of the things that you love and appreciate

    Let the feelings of love surround and fill your physical and mental body

    Read through "THE CREATIVE PROCESS FOR EXPRESSION" (pages 145-149)

    With an open heart-space and feelings of love in mind, determine:

    - How to express (slow, fast, intensely, or gently)
    - Spend some time pondering questions provided (page 148)
    - Set intentions for the project
    - Call in your higher self and spirit guides

- Set up your working space (page 144) and all supplies needed
- Create an outline of a rainbow on the canvas

    The rainbow will have seven sections to fill in with colour

    Therefore, you will need to draw eight curved lines

    Decide whether your painting will be **_landscape_** or **_portrait_** orientation

    See 'APPENDIX' – Fig. 6 on page 215

    Or disregard this if your canvas is the same length and height

    Based on the size of the canvas, determine how big each section will be

    Place the ruler vertically in the centre of the canvas

    With an H pencil, mark eight spots, evenly spaced apart

    Start from a few inches from the bottom and work upward

    These marks will be the centre point of the curved lines of the rainbow

    Now, with the H pencil, lightly draw the eight curved lines

    It does not have to be perfect

    If you make a mistake, it is okay

    Redraw the lines until you are satisfied

    The paint will cover any mistakes

    When the pencil outline is complete, trace over with a thick, black felt marker

- On a scrap piece of paper, practise painting hearts

    Use red paint, as this is the 1st colour you will be using

    Try using both the flat angled brush and the small pointy tip brush

    Or any other brush you desire

    Paint the hearts quickly

    Let them be perfectly imperfect

- Prep two shades of red acrylic paint on the palette

    On your palette, have two separate globs of red paint

    Leave one as is—red

    For the second glob, add and mix a tiny amount of white—use a palette knife

Now you have two shades of red to paint layers of hearts

Take a moment to focus on the feelings of love

Think about things you deeply love—*yourself, others, places, objects, etc.*

Let the feelings of love fill your thoughts and your body

Maybe a mantra or a string of repeated words could help hold your focus

"Love is the way, the way is love"

Or *"I am love, I am loving, and I am loved"*

Or create your own mantra from the list of things you love and appreciate

Now, start painting red hearts in the **top** curve section of the rainbow

You could start at one side and work across filling in the section

Or you could randomly jump around the whole section

First, paint larger hearts with the red

Then, paint smaller hearts with the lighter red, filling in the gaps and layering on top

Paint red hearts until the whole section is filled in

Leave the black lines showing through

Even though some of the hearts may cover parts of the black lines

Lightly spray paint with water as you work

Store any leftover paint in a sealable container

- Repeat this previous step for each colour and section of the rainbow

    For each colour, make two shades by mixing a tiny amount of white paint

    Prepare and use only one paint colour at a time

    This way the other paint will not dry out

    Below the red section, paint orange hearts

    Then, yellow hearts

    Then, green hearts

    Then, blue hearts

    Then, dark purple (indigo) hearts

    And lastly, lighter purple hearts at the bottom of the rainbow

Create the lighter purple from mixing the dark purple and lots of white

With every section, keep your focus on the feelings of love

Repeat mantras or personally chosen words of love

Lightly spray paint with water

Store any leftover paint in a sealable container as you finish each section

This project may take more than one sitting

- As sections are filled in, be aware of any emotions surfacing from focusing on feelings of love

    Maybe you feel unsettled, frustrated, or tired and need to stop

    Then walk away and leave the painting to dry

    Have a drink of water and get some fresh air

    Come back to the painting when you have had time to refresh

    Later, try again to cultivate an open heart-space and feelings of love

    Love will grow if given time and focus

    Were you able to maintain an open heart-space and feelings of love?

    Have you genuinely appreciated the magnificent power of love?

    Maybe you feel deeply connected, alive, happy, and thankful

    You could continue adding to the painting

    Use a small pointy tip brush and all seven colours

    Add tiny dots of each colour to white areas at the top and bottom of the rainbow

    Imagine they are tiny dots of love

- If the painting is finished (or you need to be finished) . . .

    Step back

    Take a moment—Breathe

    Thank your spirit guides for their help and support

    Acknowledge what you have just done

    Set your painting aside to dry completely

    Tidy up your working space and supplies

    Store any leftover paint in a sealable container

Review "AFTER WORKING ON A PROJECT" (pages 154-155)

- When the painting is dry and considered finished...

    Put it away, out of your sight—for at least a week

    Then, bring it out and *look* at it again using techniques described on page 153

    Really take some time to view and examine it

    What is your reaction to the painting now?

    Ponder the experience and thoughts from the creative process of this project

    Remember what emotion(s) you were feeling when you created your painting

    Ponder thoughts like:

    What did you feel when you created this?

    What do you feel *now* looking at it again?

    Are the feelings less intense? More intense?

    Are there other feelings surfacing?

    Does it trigger your emotions or create tension in your body?

    Do you have more to express in this piece?

    More to add or something to remove?

    Does it inspire a new project?

    Do you like the piece? Or hate it?

    Possibly do some journaling or freewriting

- Decide what to do with the painting

    It could be hung on a wall

    Or it could be given away as a gift

    It could be kept, but put away

    Or it could be discarded

    No need to rush the decision

    It could be used in the future as your feelings of love grow

Conclusion

Hopefully you now have some tools to use when you are feeling overwhelmed or when you are having a particularly hard day during this collective awakening and ascension to the 5th dimension of consciousness.

Remember . . .

- **You are not alone!**

Even if you are physically alone, higher dimensional beings of *love* and *light* are always surrounding you. Know that many others on this planet are going through the same thing, though their journeys may play out differently.

- **Do not get attached to any one technique, tool, or modality**

Our egos like to cling to and try to control pretty much everything we do. This creates judgments and opinions we then hold over ourselves, and others, continuing on the loop of karma. Try to help your ego through this time of integration by not getting attached to any of the techniques I have mentioned in this book. Try the techniques with no set outcome or schedule to follow. Use the techniques when they are needed, and leave them if they do not fit in the moment. There should be no pressure or judgment attached to a technique or modality. There should be no pressure to do it, to finish it, to be perfect at it, or to do it again. It is more about getting into the flow of what is really going on in your experience and adapting to the changes that present themselves. In the flow, we still do lots of things, just not with a strict, scheduled agenda.

- **Feel it to heal it**

Through the process of actually feeling what we are feeling, and giving it our complete focus, true release and healing has the opportunity to transpire. Make sure to stay out of the *cause* of the feelings and focus solely on the feeling itself.

- **Be easy on yourself!**

You are going to make mistakes. Mistakes are inevitable and part of the opportunity to grow and expand our consciousness. It is not about being perfect, but instead, it is about how you deal with something and move forward after mistakes are made. It is important to focus on your *response* to circumstances, rather than the circumstances themselves. Try to learn something from your mistakes, either about your own inner reality or the people and the world you find yourself in. Our mistakes can be viewed as life lessons we have the opportunity to learn and expand from. So, be easy on yourself; it is all a part of the process.

- **Support the physical and emotional body**

There will be good days when you feel rested, motivated, energetic, and inspired. There will also be hard days, when you are exhausted, lonely, unmotivated, and lack inspiration. Love yourself through it all! Try to *go with the flow*. On the good days, get stuff done on your to-do list, offer help and support to others, express gratitude and appreciation, and do something that brings you joy. On the hard days, surrender to the intensity, take special care of your emotional and physical body, leave things that can be done another day, and try some of the tools I have expressed in this book.

- **Make some healthy changes**

First, there is the realization that changes need to be made, and secondly, there is the actual act of making changes in your daily life. Both of these steps are not the easiest things to do, but they are well worth the work in the long run. Part of the awakening is the process of getting back to our authentic selves and embracing a healthier emotional and physical state of being. We are divine beings, and thus need to treat ourselves with the utmost love and respect. A good place to start would be taking a deep look at:

- What you put **into** your body
- What you put **on** your body
- What you put **around** your body
- What judgments do you hold for yourself? For others?
- What are your internal conversations focused on?
- What are your beliefs and opinions? What are they based on?
- What do you identify with? Why?
- What do you avoid, turn away from, or neglect?

Taking a really close look at yourself has the ability to open your perspective on the current circumstances you find yourself in. Peeling away the layers of things we identify with may eventually lead us back to our pristine origins. Try to focus on yourself and the changes you need to make, and let others worry about themselves. We do not need to change anybody else, but instead show through our own actions how changes can be embraced.

- **Build up your self-confidence and self-love**

It all starts within us, the changes we want to see in our lives and the world. We need to cultivate love and respect for ourselves and remember just how sacred every living being is. So, take some time every day to acknowledge your sacredness and divinity, and love who you are now—all the parts.

- **The ebb and flow of awakening**

There is a time for gaining knowledge, having experiences, and interacting with others. Then, there is a time for integration where we require time to process and ponder the gained knowledge, experiences, and interactions alone in our own internal space. Follow your intuition and the subtle synchronicities in your life to determine whether it is a time for acquiring experiences and knowledge or a time for integration and stillness.

- **Tune out from mainstream media**

Avoid as much news, social media, outside opinions, and ideas as possible in your daily life. Try to let go of the outside story playing out and, rather, focus on your own personal story. You are the main character of your experience, therefore make *you* the main focus. Trust your intuition and know that you will know what you need to know, when you need to know it. Look outside your window and the community around; this is your reality, more so than what you are seeing on a screen. Reconnect to the natural world and your connection to it.

- **Spread your love and light**

So many people feel unworthy, unloved, and in pain, especially at this time of the collective awakening. So much hidden unprocessed pain and suffering is surfacing, and everyone is feeling the pressure. This is a time to *hold space* and send beams of love from your heart chakra to humanity and Mother Earth. Wherever you see pain and suffering, send love. To all the "negative" people in the world, send love. They need it the most, and your love may even protect and prevent their future victims from harm.

The way is love. Love is the way.

From my heart to yours.

Acknowledgements

I would deeply like to thank my husband, Al, and my daughter, Aydan, for inspiring me to create this book. They encouraged, supported, and loved me through this adventure. And what an adventure it was!

Thank you to the beautiful Mother Earth and divine Universe for providing a space for so much to unfold.

Thank you to all my spirit guides for their patience, guidance, support and unconditional love.

Thank you to **all** the beautiful Souls upon, around, and in this planet.

And, with the utmost respect, I acknowledge and celebrate the K'ómoks First Nation whose unceded territory I learn, live, work and play on.

APPENDIX

PROJECT #5

Fig. 1

PROJECT #6

Fig. 2

PROJECT #7

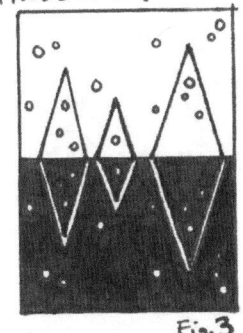

Fig. 3

PROJECT #8

Fig. 4

PROJECT #9

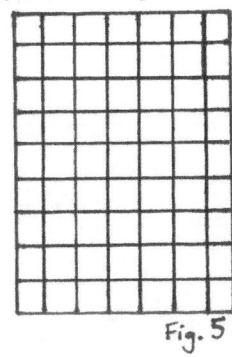

Fig. 5

PROJECT #10

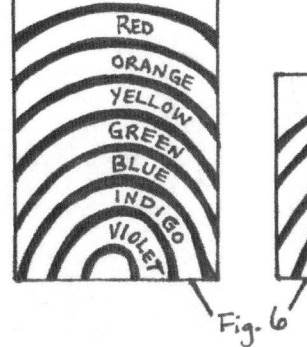

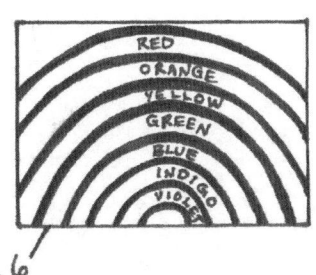

Fig. 6

PORTRAIT ORIENTATION

LANDSCAPE ORIENTATION

Bibliography

Brown, Christina. *The Book of Yoga*. Bath, UK: Parragon, 2003. Print.

Chapman, Gary. *The 5 Love Languages: the Secrets to Love That Lasts*. Chicago, IL: Northfield Publishing, 2010. Print.

D'Alleva, Anne. *Methods & Theories of Art History*. London, UK: Laurence King Publishing Ltd., 2012. Print.

DeMeo, James. *The Orgone Accumulator Handbook*. Ashlad, OR: Natural Energy Works, 2010. Print.

Dr. Farmer, Steven. *Pocket Guide to Spirit Animals: Understanding Messages from your Animal Spirit Guides*. USA: Hay House, Inc., 2012. Print.

Dr. Milanovich, Norma J., Cynthia Ploski and Betty Rice. *We, the Arcturians*. Kalispell, MT: Athena Publishing, 1990. Print.

Fersen, Eugene. *Science of Being*. Collegedale, TN: The Light Bearers Publishing, LLC, 2011. Print.

Freeland, Cynthia. *But is it Art?* New York, NY: Oxford University Press Inc., 2001. Print.

Frost, S. E. *Basic Teachings of the Great Philosophers*. New York, NY: Doubleday Dell Publishing Group, Inc., 1989. Print.

Glasson, Natalie Sian. *White Beacons of Atlantis*. Flagstaff, AZ: Light Technology Publishing, 2015. Print.

Haich, Elisabeth. *Initiation*. Santa Fe, NM: Aurora Press Inc., 2000. Print.

Hof, Wim. *The Wim Hof Method*. Louisville, CO: Sounds True, Inc., 2020. Print.

Judith, Anodea. *Wheels of Life*. MN, USA: Llewellyn Publications, 2016. Print.

Kahn, Matt. *Everything is here to Help You: A Loving Guide to Your Soul's Evolution*. USA: Hay House Inc., 2018. Print.

Kahn, Matt. *The Universe Always Has a Plan: 10 Golden Rules of Letting Go*. USA: Hay House Inc., 2020. Print.

Kahn, Matt. *Whatever Arises, Love That: A Love Revolution That Begins With You*. Boulder, CO: Sounds True, Inc., 2016. Print.

Luna, Luis Eduardo and Pablo Amaringo. *Ayahuasca Visions: The Religious Iconography of a Peruvian Shaman*. Berkeley, CA: North Atlantic Books, 1999. Print.

Matthews, Caitlin. *Singing the Soul Back Home: Shamanic Wisdom for Every Day*. London, UK: Connections Book Publishing Limited, 2002. Print.

Megre, Vladimir. *Anastasia*. Kahului, HI: Ringing Cedar Press, 2008. Print.

Megre, Vladimir. *The Ringing Cedars of Russia*. Kahului, HI: Ringing Cedar Press, 2008. Print.

Megre, Vladimir. *The Space of Love*. Kahului, HI: Ringing Cedar Press, 2008. Print.

Megre, Vladimir. *Co-creation*. Kahului, HI: Ringing Cedar Press, 2008. Print.

Megre, Vladimir. *Who Are We?* Kahului, HI: Ringing Cedar Press, 2008. Print.

Megre, Vladimir. *The Book of Kin*. Kahului, HI: Ringing Cedar Press, 2008. Print.

Megre, Vladimir. *The Energy of Life*. Kahului, HI: Ringing Cedar Press, 2008. Print.

Megre, Vladimir. *The New Civilisation*. Kahului, HI: Ringing Cedar Press, 2008. Print.

Megre, Vladimir. *Rites of Love*. Kahului, HI: Ringing Cedar Press, 2008. Print.

Miller, David K. *Connecting With the Arcturians*. Flagstaff, AZ: Light Technology Publishing, 2016. Print.

Penczak, Christopher. *Spirit Allies: Meet Your Team from the Other Side*. San Francisco, CA: Red Wheel/Weiser, 2002. Print.

Redfield, James. *The Celestine Prophecy: An Adventure*. New York, NY: Warner Books Inc., 1993. Print.

Redfield, James and Carol Adrienne. *The Celestine Prophecy: An Experiential Guide*. New York, NY: Warner Books Inc., 1995. Print.

Redfield, James. *The Celestine Vision: Living the New Spiritual Awareness*. New York, NY: Warner Books Inc., 1997. Print.

Redfield, James. *The Tenth Insight: Holding the Vision*. New York, NY: Warner Books Inc., 1996. Print.

Redmond, Layne. *Chakra Meditation: Transformation through the Seven Energy Centers of the Body*. Boulder, CA: Sounds True Inc., 2010. Print.

Roberts, Jane. *Seth Speaks: The Eternal Validity of the Soul*. New York, NY: Bantam, 1980. Print.

Roberts, Jane. *The Nature of Personal Reality: Specific, Practical Techniques for Solving Everyday Problems and Enriching the Life You Know*. Emeryville, CA: Publishers Group West, 1994. Print.

Rosen, Stanley. *The Philosopher's Handbook*. New York, NY: Random House Inc., 2000. Print.

Ruiz, Don Miguel. *The Four Agreements: A Practical Guide to Personal Freedom*. San Rafael, CA: Amber-Allen Publishing, 1997. Print.

Spalding, Tina Louise. *Jesus: My Autobiography*. Flagstaff, AZ: Light Technology Publishing, 2015. Print.

Thetford, William T. and Helen Schucman. *A Course in Miracles*. Omaha, NE: Course in Miracles Society, 2012. Print.

Tolle, Eckhart. *A New Earth: Awakening to Your Life's Purpose*. New York, NY: Dutton/Penguin Group, 2005. Print.

Tolle, Eckhart. *The Power of Now*. Vancouver, BC: Namaste Publishing Inc., 2004. Print.

Wilcock, David. *The Source Field Investigations: The Hidden Science and Last Civilizations behind the 2012 Prophecies*. New York, NY: Dutton, 2016. Print.

Endnotes

Introduction

1   Gibran, Kahlil. *The Prophet*. Toronto, ON: Random House of Canada Limited, 2008. Page 52.

2   Thoreau, Henry David. *Walden*. London, UK: Arcturus Publishing Limited, 2020. Page 143.

3   Tolle, Eckhart. *The Power of Now*. Vancouver, BC: Namaste Publishing Inc., 2004. Page 22.

4   Judith, Anodea. *Wheels of Life*. MN, USA: Llewellyn Publications, 2016. Page 4.

Printed in Canada